Jossey-Bass Teacher

Jossey-Bass Teacher provides educators with practical knowledge and tools to create a positive and lifelong impact on student learning. We offer classroom-tested and research-based teaching resources for a variety of grade levels and subject areas. Whether you are an aspiring, new, or veteran teacher, we want to help you make every teaching day your best.

From ready-to-use classroom activities to the latest teaching framework, our value-packed books provide insightful, practical, and comprehensive materials on the topics that matter most to K–12 teachers. We hope to become your trusted source for the best ideas from the most experienced and respected experts in the field.

JUN 08   CH

The Homeschooling
BOOK OF LISTS

MICHAEL LEPPERT and
MARY LEPPERT

JOSSEY-BASS
A Wiley Imprint
www.josseybass.com

Published by Jossey-Bass
A Wiley Imprint
989 Market Street, San Francisco, CA 94103-1741—www.josseybass.com

Jossey-Bass books and products are available through most bookstores. To contact Jossey-Bass directly call our Customer Care Department within the U.S. at 800-956-7739, outside the U.S. at 317-572-3986, or fax 317-572-4002.

Jossey-Bass also publishes its books in a variety of electronic formats. Some content that appears in print may not be available in electronic books.

Library of Congress Cataloging-in-Publication Data

Leppert, Michael.
    The homeschooling book of lists / Michael and Mary Leppert.
      p. cm.
    Includes index.
    ISBN-13: 978-0-7879-9671-0 (alk. paper)
      1. Home schooling—Handbooks, manuals, etc. I. Leppert, Mary. II. Title.
    LC40.L48 2008
    371.04'2—dc22
                                                      2007047364

Printed in the United States of America
FIRST EDITION
PB Printing 10 9 8 7 6 5 4 3 2 1

About This Book

Homeschooling—yikes! Scary! No, it isn't. With *The Homeschooling Book of Lists*, you can see through the mists of myth surrounding this fast-growing alternative to public school and see if homeschooling is a good fit for your family. We have written this book to take the anxiety and guesswork out of teaching your children at home, for whatever reasons you may have—religious, social, academic, parents' unusual work patterns, travel—all of the reasons families have for homeschooling.

The book provides a wealth of useful information for new or veteran homeschoolers. You'll find lists of products, resources, and curricula that will help you teach your child and enjoy the process along the way. We will discuss the pitfalls, peaks, and valleys that all homeschoolers experience—including skeptical family and friends, socialization, different learning styles and methods, and college admissions—and we'll give you strategies to deal with them. We've also added a section with coupons in the back to help you save money and launch your career as a home-teacher.

So, come on, dive in! We hope you find this book useful, and we welcome you to visit us at www.homeschoolnewslink.com.

The Authors

Michael and Mary Leppert have been married for twenty-eight years. They have one son, Lennon, twenty, who has been homeschooled all of his life.

Before becoming parents, the Lepperts worked in marketing, printing, and publishing. After Lennon was born in 1987, Mary ventured into homeschooling while researching various aspects of alternative education. In 1995, the Lepperts began publishing *The Link* Homeschool Newspaper, which has become the nation's largest all-inclusive homeschool publication. They also publish five websites, on topics ranging from parenting to choral singing.

Co-authors of *Homeschooling Almanac, 2002–2003* (Prima, 2001), the Lepperts produce their own annual conference for the homeschooling community and present workshops at other homeschool conventions around the country.

You may contact them with any questions or comments at link.art@verizon .net, or visit them online at any of their websites:

- The Link: www.homeschoolnewslink.com
- Autonomous Parenting: www.autonomousparenting.com
- The Link Homeschool Conference: www.californiahomeschoolconference .com
- Teacher's Round: www.teachersround.com
- 21st Century Chorister: www.21stcenturychorister.com

*We wish to dedicate this book to all of
the homeschooling parents who have exhibited
the courage, exerted the effort, and stuck with
this wonderful way to live and raise children.
It takes courage and strength to go against the grain.
Thank you.*

*We also wish to dedicate this book to our
own wonderful homeschooled person, our son
Lennon Leppert, who is such a joy to know
and a source of constant pride and happiness.
To paraphrase Carly Simon: "From the moment
we first saw you, the second that you were born . . .
we knew that you were the love of our lives."*

—Michael and Mary Leppert

Acknowledgments

We wish to take this opportunity to recognize a number of the pioneers who have shaped the homeschooling world we all live in today. The late Dr. Raymond and Dorothy Moore, whose books—based on their studies of childhood learning and development—have brought relief and guidance to hundreds of parents who worried that their children were not learning early enough or fast enough. David and Micki Colfax, also authors of two excellent books, homeschooled their four sons and ultimately saw them accepted into Harvard and Yale, making a comfortable "poster family" for all of us to point to proudly, when skeptics and critics asked homeschoolers "What about college?" John Taylor Gatto, the thirty-year veteran of Manhattan public schools, whose books, articles, and lectures have shed tremendous light on the very nature of public schooling and its use as a tool of social engineering. Diane Flynn Keith, homeschooling mom of two grown sons, popular author, regular columnist and editor of *Homefires* and *Clickschooling*, for her humor, intelligent insight, and innovations in the homeschooling world. The late John Holt and his right-hand assistant, Pat Farenga, who has served as president of Holt Associates since John's passing. Pat's books, articles, and lectures have also spread a vast amount of light and inspiration to those who wish to have their children "grow without schooling." David Albert, homeschooling dad, author, and book publisher, who was the first to publish John Taylor Gatto's seminal book *Dumbing Us Down*. Richard Prystowsky, homeschooling father, college professor, regular columnist, and conference lecturer, whose Jewish-Buddhist (often humorous) observations about life, family, and homeschooling provide welcome guidance to all of us homeschooling outside of the usual realm—sometimes making it up as we go! Catherine Levison, one of the top experts on Charlotte Mason education and author of two superb books on the topic, who has given so many families guidance and support over the last fifteen years. Martin and Carolyn Forte, homeschooling parents of two grown daughters and owners of a Southern California–based independent study program and website, who have provided many years of instruction, writing, lecturing, and general goodwill to all those who come to them. Dr. Mary Hood, who has successfully bridged the gap between Christian and non-Christian homeschoolers with her humorous and sensible books, lectures, and overall guidance in her Georgia resource center. Andrew Pudewa, a homeschooling father of six and a vital and brilliant teacher of creative writing, whose lectures and DVDs ease many a parent's worried mind. And finally, but not least, learning styles coaches and experts Mariaemma Pelullo-Willis and Victoria Kindle-Hodson, whose "Learning Styles Profile" completely changed how we looked at homeschooling for all three of us, and who have been at every conference since 1997 and write a regular column for *The Link*. To all of these wonderful people, we say "Thank you for going ahead of us and being such a great influence to us and so many other homeschooling families!"

These are not all of the people we could list, of course, but the ones we have been most communicative with and were greatly influenced by, as we became conscious of the world of homeschooling. All across the country, there are people who are intelligent and sensitive and who work hard to produce books, lectures, articles, radio programs, magazines, and websites that serve homeschoolers well—we wish to acknowledge them, too, even though not individually. We are proud to be in your company and call ourselves homeschoolers!

We would also like to thank all the parents across the United States and around the world who take the often difficult plunge into homeschooling.

On a personal level, we wish to give a warm thank-you and extend our deep appreciation to our office staff of *The Link*: Kyle Zook, our lead graphic designer, a superb writer and resident intellectual, who designed and composed the book coupons, as well as researched and did the initial drafting of many of the science entries; Linda Foster, another "brain" who is the best reviewer and analyst we have ever seen, who researched and drafted some of the other product sections; and Sylvia Bardelli, whose warmth and attention to detail is indispensable in helping develop the coupons, aiding us in our research and proofing, and also holding down the office while we took the time to write this book.

On the book-production level: in writing any book, no matter how well one knows the subject matter, it is easy to lose sight of one's objective from time to time. The invaluable assistance of the highly skilled and patient staff of Jossey-Bass is greatly appreciated by both of us. Margie McAneny, our chief editor, for her constant oversight and gentle steering of our project; Julia Parmer, who assisted Margie and helped us with the organization of the book; Lesley Iura, who helped to shepherd this project while Margie was out on maternity leave; Dimi Berkner, who was an early champion of this book idea; Chris Wallace, who created such a beautiful cover for the book; and Justin Frahm, who turned our manuscript into a finished book.

Last, we wish to acknowledge our beloved son, Lennon, who works with us and helps us every day and who made homeschooling possible—and necessary!

Contents

Preface

We have been immersed in homeschooling for nearly two decades. Our nineteen-year-old son, Lennon, was taught at home all of his life. We lived in a number of different states in his early years, and as we took him to homeschooling park days and other social activities in religious and nonreligious support groups, we realized that there are many great products, cultural practices, and writers completely suitable to both religious and nonreligious homeschoolers. However, most families were not aware of them because at that time the groups remained insulated from each other.

In 1995, we began *The Link* in an attempt to link together the religious and nonreligious worlds of homeschooling. *The Link* was immediately distributed nationwide, to friends and support groups we had known in these early years of Lennon's life, and it has grown tremendously since then. Our website (www .homeschoolnewslink.com) and e-newsletter *The Way Home* now serve the homeschooling world electronically as well.

Publishing *The Link* and our electronic products, as well as producing twelve homeschool conferences in Los Angeles and Greensboro, North Carolina, since 1997, has kept us active and involved in the broad community of homeschoolers. Hearing from our newspaper's readership, as well as talking face to face with parents who attend our conferences, provides us with a broad foundation of knowledge about homeschooling and the issues that are important to parents and children.

In this book we'd like to share this information and wisdom with you. Whether you are a religious homeschooler or not, an experienced homeschooler or a parent just toying with the idea of educating your child at home, we hope this book will provide you with all the information you need to do it happily and with satisfaction.

How to Use This Book

This book is designed to help you find products, services, and resources to assist you in homeschooling your child.

Part One will provide you with helpful background information to consider before you begin homeschooling. Of particular note in this section are the Frequently Asked Questions about Homeschooling and the Glossary of Common Terms. The FAQs answer virtually any general question you have about homeschooling, and the Glossary will prove useful in broadening your knowledge of the homeschooling world.

There are a variety of ways to teach your child at home, ranging from a classical education to more modern techniques like the delayed academic approach. Part Two, Homeschooling Models and Methods, provides a good overview of these many approaches to homeschooling, so that you can choose those that best suit your family.

Part Three, Subjects and Lesson Plans, points out resources and curricula available to homeschoolers on every academic subject imaginable—from language arts, math, astronomy, and civics to art history. In Part Four, Homeschooling Resources, you will find more specialized sources of information for homeschooling. This section covers everything from religious homeschooling resources (including Christian, Jewish, and Islamic) to independent study programs as well as educating a child with special needs.

A big question for many homeschoolers is, "What about college?" Many homeschooled students go on to attend institutions from Harvard and Yale to community colleges—there are even a large number of colleges and universities who actively seek out students who have been educated at home. Part Five, Getting Your Homeschooled Student into College, provides everything you need to know about this phase of your child's education, from college admissions and transcripts to distance learning options for higher education.

The appendices will provide you with a wealth of useful resources for homeschooling. You can turn to Appendix A, Homeschooling State by State, to find information on homeschooling in your home state. (Once you have found this, you should look over your state's legal requirements for homeschooling. We cannot give specific legal advice; only an attorney can do so.) Depending on your state, you should choose the statewide parents' group that appeals to you, go to their website, and find a contact person in your area, if possible. That person typically can provide insight into what it is *really* like to homeschool in your state. Often the state requirements that are on paper are more stringent than the actual practice.

Appendix B, Where to Go for More Information, lists useful magazines and books for homeschool families. Appendix C, Who's Who in Homeschooling, will help you become familiar with prominent names in the homeschooling world as well as in the broader field of education. Appendix D, Sample Transcript for College Admission, provides invaluable assistance to you and your child with the college admissions process. Appendix E, Coupons, contains valuable discounts and other cost-saving opportunities for homeschoolers.

Homeschooling is fun and fulfilling—as well as a serious parenting endeavor and a large commitment that will test you every so often. But with this book and your own initiative and native intelligence, you can do it. Good luck!

Part One

Things to Consider Before Homeschooling

Homeschooling Is Not About Religion

No matter what our philosophical background or beliefs may be, we can recognize the fact that humans are mammals, and mammal parents raise their young, teaching them life skills and the ways of the species until a level of life independence is reached and the offspring can survive and thrive on their own.

In this regard, human parents have the responsibility to teach and raise their young to this point of life independence. Therefore, the greatest benefit parents can provide their children is to be the teachers of academic as well as life skills, providing seamless continuity. What brings many people to homeschooling is a psychological "tap on the shoulder" that leads them to realize that they want to nurture and care for their children's education, for the child's peace of mind, safety, and success.

Such a "tap" can come from a bully at school, a drug problem in the school system, a lack of academic progress by their child, or a myriad of other situations. To provide safety, security, and total focus to the child's learning experience, these distractions are best removed from the child's world. Plus, each family is a sovereign entity, with its culture and background unique. Children benefit from having this uniqueness celebrated and nurtured.

Many people assume that homeschooling is a religious activity. This is due to the fact that in the early 1980s (the beginning of the "modern era" of homeschooling) most homeschooling families were doing so for religious reasons—the demise of prayer in public schools, presence of sex education, teaching of the theory of evolution as proven scientific fact—all made many religious parents wish to remove their children from the atmosphere of public, government-controlled institutions and teach them at home, using religious materials that conformed to the parents' belief system.

Since the late 1990s, the majority of growth in homeschooling has come from families who choose to homeschool not for religious reasons, but for scholastic reasons or social reasons—to prevent bullying, for instance, or to provide their children with a quiet and peaceful environment in which to study and learn. Academically, for instance, homeschooling provides the opportunity for gifted children to move quickly through grade school and high school and begin college work in the early teens. But even if the child is not gifted, his or her chances of academic success are enhanced by homeschooling.

Of course, the ranks of religious homeschoolers still grow—Christian, Jewish, and Muslim parents all wish to teach their children by their own religious and cultural guidelines, and more products than ever are available for these families. But homeschooling is not the domain of religious zealots. Many homeschooling parents are professional people or have degrees and secondary degrees. They recognize the tremendous benefits—both academic and social—that homeschooling affords their children and the family as a whole.

List 1.1. Reasons to Homeschool

The first reasons to homeschool are *family*-related reasons.

- *Independence.* Homeschooling helps children achieve the adult state of life independence.
- *Individuality.* Homeschooling nurtures the child's uniqueness. Individuality is promoted and enhanced so that each child develops high self-esteem and realization of his or her unique place in the world.
- *Healthy social environment.* Homeschooling provides a social environment that is free from bullying and other distractions; the child can concentrate 100 percent on his schoolwork and then play or socialize.
- *Strong family bonds.* Homeschooling promotes and develops a strong, healthy bond between parents and children.
- *No more school time-clock.* Homeschooling removes the tyranny of the institutional school time-clock from the home and family. This decreases stress and anxiety.

The next reasons to homeschool are *academic*:

- *The teacher-student ratio is one-to-one.* Even if there are many children in the family, the teaching parent has to address only one child at a time and can control the environment more comfortably. Plus, children at home are not usually disrupted and distracted as often as in a school setting.
- *Less time wasted.* In homeschooling, all of the academic study time is spent on that study.
- *Less time is required for teaching.* On average, more can be accomplished in two to three hours of homeschooling per day than in six hours in the classroom. (According to Dr. Oliver DeMille, "The actual curriculum of the public school system is about 75% social and 25% skills" (*The Link,* Vol. 6, Issue 3).
- *Earlier college entrance.* Many homeschooled students begin attending college at a much younger age than their age peers who attend institutional schools. This is due to the fact that most community colleges allow dual enrollment by high school students, but homeschoolers have more flexible time available to attend these classes, whereas public high school students must attend on nights or weekends.
- *Increase in standardized test scores.* In the ten years from 1994 to 2004, homeschoolers tended to score 15 percentile points higher, on average, than their age-peers who are not homeschooled. This is true for the

ACT, as well—according to the Homeschool Legal Defense Association (www.hslda.org), "In 2004 the 7,858 homeschool students taking the ACT scored an average of 22.6, compared to the national average of 20.9."

- *Maximizes academic achievement and increases self-esteem for each individual child.* If a child does not respond well to a particular book, program, or approach, it can be changed quickly for the child's benefit, before the child is stressed and her self-esteem is damaged. In school, such rapid response to a poor fit is not possible, and the negative effects damage the child.
- *Special needs flexibility.* The academic flexibility provided by homeschooling is even more apparent with a child who has learning disabilities or special needs.
- *Individualized delivery of information.* Homeschooling provides the child with the opportunity to have information delivered at his own pace, rather than by the classroom average.
- *Homeschooling delivers in a steady flow, and the child never stops learning.* The child learns that her brain is always "on"; that even when she is not reading a book or doing a lesson, she is still learning. Therefore, information is a steady flow—whether doing academic work or grocery shopping. Homeschooling families often teach math via shopping, cooking, and other nonacademic avenues.
- *Nurturance of children's natural curiosity.* Children are curious by nature, and this quality tends to be nurtured and promoted by homeschooling. They learn things because they are curious about them, interested in them.

The third reason to homeschool involves *social* considerations:

- *Protection from bullying and peer pressure.* Homeschooling eliminates schoolyard bullying and much peer-group pressure and also eliminates racial or ethnic friction during learning.
- *Eliminates drug influences and other negative social aspects.* Homeschooling helps children avoid these negative influences now associated with the schoolyard.
- *Creates optimum learning atmosphere.* Homeschooling creates a quiet and safe environment for the child, allowing him to focus fully on learning. This in turn eliminates stress and anxiety, which can also block memory and learning.
- *An abundance of positive socialization.* School does not provide much healthy socialization: on average, little more than one hour of social

activity per day. Most positive age-peer interaction for the school child occurs in her own neighborhood or in extracurricular activities like Scouting and sports. Homeschooling offers children the opportunity to truly socialize with other people—not only children their own age, but those younger and older, and adults as well. On average, this creates a more well-rounded social individual and more closely resembles the social atmosphere of adult life.

List 1.2. Reasons Not to Homeschool

For someone who believes that homeschooling is the best way to teach and raise children, this is a difficult list to develop. In our years of experience, we have seen and heard of a few reasons why a family would choose not to homeschool.

- *Parental learning disability.* If you, the parent, have a true learning disability that interferes with your own processing of academic information, and you don't see teaching your child as a way to overcome it, then you may not want to homeschool.
- *Parental lack of patience.* If you *really* do not have the patience to teach your own child and do not want to develop it, then you may not want to homeschool. This may require a significant amount of self-reflection, of course.
- *Home location.* If you live in an out-of-the-way area and feel that your child cannot successfully participate in the social activities around your locale, or if there are none, then you may not want to homeschool.
- *A satisfactory school district.* If you believe your local school system does well by your child and you do not believe that you can do better—or need to—you may not want to homeschool.
- *A responsive school district.* If your local school district has an attitude of service to the parents of its students and listens to their concerns and responds quickly and reasonably, you almost have an extended homeschooling situation already.
- *Work responsibilities away from home.* If you are a single parent and must work outside of home to make a living, you may not want to homeschool.
- *A lack of extracurricular benefits, such as organized sports, proms, and so on.* Many homeschoolers are not able to enjoy these aspects of institutional schooling, although there are regions where homeschoolers have well-organized sports networks, and some support groups sponsor proms, graduations, science fairs, and the like. There are also school districts that are required to allow homeschoolers to participate in organized sports and some other extracurricular activities, as long as they meet the same qualifications as the regular school students.

List 1.3. What to Expect If Your Child Is Already in School

This is by far the more difficult situation for homeschooling—at least in the beginning. Each school district receives Average Daily Attendance (ADA) funds for each child, each day the child is in school. The districts do not appreciate losing this ADA money due to a child's being homeschooled. Therefore you should use extra care in notifying the district in writing that your child will be "transferring" to homeschooling. You will likely also experience some of the following:

- *Increased reporting requirements* to the school district. Most states require parents who remove their children from school to file a report—when the removal occurs and usually each year at the beginning of the school year—attesting that the child is being homeschooled.
- *A period of "decompression"* in which your child may be unruly, out-of-sorts, agitated, or the like. This is because the child is most likely coming from a comparatively "hostile" environment, in which children are one-upping and criticizing each other on a daily basis or seeking the approval of the teacher at the expense of other students. For your child, this has created the need for a sound defense mechanism that becomes unnecessary when the child is at home and away from the pressures of impressing others and protecting herself from barbs.

  This transition will take some time; many expert homeschoolers suggest that you let your child take a month off *just to be with you.* Take this opportunity to go to museums or on short trips, and allow yourselves to get to know each other better. After decompression is over, you can begin academics in earnest, usually with a child whose attitude is positive and enthusiastic.
- *Less time on academics, more time on life.* Your child will not be spending six or more hours in class each day and won't have mountains of homework every night, so he will be able to begin to develop more outside interests and become a more well-rounded person and a true individual. Two to four hours per day is plenty of study time for the sixth to ninth grader. Then you may have to devote a little more time per day from tenth to twelfth grade, especially as the child nears graduation, because of lab work and other such work, but certainly there won't be six hours, day in and day out, taken up with schooling.
- *Record-keeping.* You will now be responsible for maintaining attendance records, academic completion records, and transcripts. Some states require this record-keeping, but even if your state does not

require it, you will probably want to be able to create transcripts for college admissions requirements when the time comes. It is difficult to recall exactly what your child did three or four years in the past, so it is best to track as you go. (For more on this transcript creation, see List 5.2 and Appendix D.)

- *You are the problem-solver now.* If your child has difficulty in an academic area, you will be the person who has to come up with a solution. Don't worry; there are excellent tutors available online (see List 4.9, Tutors and Tutoring) and—depending on where you live—locally, too. However, you won't have a teacher to fall back on as you did before, unless you are enrolled in an independent study program (ISP) or charter school. (See List 4.7, Charter Schools and Independent Study Programs.)

Often a problem goes unaddressed in school until it is "too late" for remedial help to be of sufficient use. The time to correct a problem with a college-entrance-required math or science course is not when the college applications are being sent out, but far enough in advance to help your child feel confident of her ability to handle the subject. When you are the problem-solver, you can take advantage of the opportunity to resolve the problem with your child when it first arises.

List 1.4. Frequently Asked Questions About Homeschooling

In our roles as newspaper publishers and editors, conference sponsors, and homeschooling parents, we frequently talk with dozens of other homeschooling parents, and children too. We are also asked questions by (usually) anxious parents who want to homeschool their children, but are very unsure of this brave new world, so foreign to most of them and their relatives. Although this list of FAQs cannot cover every single question you may have, it will definitely cover the main ones and may shed light on some others for you, as well.

Q What about socialization?

 A Because this is by far the most frequently asked question, we have placed it first. Just consider for a moment that in the average school day of six hours, your child spends approximately one-and-a-half hours "socializing": two fifteen-minute recesses and one hour at lunch. The rest of the time the child usually sits at his desk, separated from the other children by the invisible wall of "good behavior." Plus, as the school atmosphere becomes increasingly restricted and dangerous, the socialization that occurs is not the healthy kind that fosters interpersonal skills, but in some schools is becoming more akin to the atmosphere in a correctional institution.

 Homeschooling parents that we speak with often report that their children have nearly too much socialization; we have had the same experience. We attend weekly park days; a vast number of field trips; gym and karate classes; skate days or hiking treks. Besides planned events, children who live in urban or suburban areas run errands with their mom or dad and come into contact with people all day long in supermarkets and the like. A child's playmates live in her neighborhood, just as they always have, and whether they are homeschooled or attend school, your child will have plenty of interaction with them.

 Families in rural areas have always had to take extra steps to make sure that their children came into contact with other children beyond the school hours. Today's rural families are no different, and homeschoolers simply have to make the same arrangements the schooled kids have to make. The simple fact is that children who are taught at home have *more* time to socialize in a healthy, humane, and free fashion, without the intrusion of "authority" figures shaping their every move. One does not develop social skills by having a teacher monitor the play or talk, but by self-directed playing and talking with other children and adults.

Q What about critical or skeptical family members?

A Usually a skeptical family member has concerns about academic and socialization issues. If you read your skeptics who express doubts about socialization the preceding Q&A, it may start them thinking about this very significant topic. Parents in urban areas who have had occasion to drop by a junior high or middle school in the middle of the day and see it in "lockdown" mode know that school socialization is not necessarily desirable or healthy. Also, those family members who do not live with your child may not have the opportunity to see the positive changes he experiences once he is no longer in the public school environment. Try inviting the skeptic in your family to accompany you on park days or field trips so they can see firsthand what your child's daily life is really like.

We know about this issue from our own experience with Michael's mother, who was very skeptical when she first heard our plans to homeschool. When school enrollment time came and went, and we didn't have Lennon in school, she was worried and offered to buy our first-grade boxed curriculum. She also came to Los Angeles for a visit from Chicago and accompanied Lennon and Mary on our routine the first week of her visit.

I, Mary, remember the week as clearly as if it were yesterday. Monday began with a field trip to the J. Paul Getty Art Museum. Tuesday was homeschool gymnastics class at a top-notch Olympic training gym facility (with about fifteen other families); on Wednesday Lennon had his beginning Yamaha Music School class (with ten other children who weren't homeschoolers); Thursday was a park day (with twenty to forty other homeschooled children, playing for approximately four hours without a fight or other negative incident); Friday was Lennon's chorus rehearsal at the Yamaha School (with twenty-five nonhomeschooled children). Our son was occupied with trips to the library, doing his schoolwork in the early mornings, and listening to Michael read to all of us in the evenings. Michael's mother quickly realized that not only was her grandson *not* socially deprived, but he had a culturally and academically rich life, filled with wonderful people, music, chorus, gymnastics—training he would not receive in a school setting. After her visit, we heard from relatives that she spoke with much pride about what a great life Lennon had!

Q What if all my child's friends are schooled and she feels "different"?

A Once upon a time we would have answered this question by suggesting that parents do little things like buy a lunch pail and pencil and paper pads at the beginning of each school year and try to incorporate more "school-type" things into your lives to make your child feel like she was "fitting in." Now we would suggest that you remind your child how fortunate she is to be homeschooled, and what a privilege it is to be learning in such a rich and enjoyable atmosphere. Over the years, our son has taught us that we should be proud to be homeschoolers, that we should feel different because we are. We view his sense of pride in being homeschooled as righteous and healthy. In today's society, there is constant talk about building self-esteem in children, but often people confuse this with having the child wear a T-shirt that says "I'm Great!" Strong self-esteem is built not from words but from actions. If you knew that homeschooling your child would give her a tremendous sense of self-esteem—far beyond what she would gain in a school— would you do it? Foster the difference and be proud of it!

Q What if my child goes back to school? Will the school accept him?

A The law in all fifty states is that children who are U.S. citizens cannot be denied public education unless they have been legally expelled or there is some other extenuating circumstance. Therefore, the more likely phrasing of this question is, "What is the easiest way to get my child back into school after he or she has been homeschooled?" The answer depends on which state you live in. If you declare your homeschool a private school, then it is crucial to keep good records of daily activities and the subjects studied, should you eventually decide to enroll your child in school. If you enroll in an independent study program (ISP), either privately or through a public school, you will have no problems transferring back into the system. (In some states, an ISP is called a *church school.*) Call your state's parent-run state organization (see Appendix A) for in-depth information.

Q What if my child does not want to leave his school friends?

A This can be a very tough and unexpected situation to face. It often comes up when we talk with parents who choose to homeschool not because of academic issues but because of the negative peer pressure their child experiences at school. In our observations and discussions with parents, it seems that most children, when removed from a negative school environment, feel a sense of relief—a sense of having been rescued, if you will, from something they were partially attracted to but uncomfortable with. If you have taught your child powerful moral and ethical awareness, the inner turmoil that comes as a result of the peer-group temptation and his inner sense of rightness can cause a great deal of stress. Relieving him of this stress is a wonderful thing. Homeschooling doesn't mean you are moving to another planet!

There are still after-school hours and weekends that allow plenty of time for children to continue seeing school friends they like.

Q How will I know if a particular homeschool group is right for me and my child?

A Fitting into a homeschool group and having it fit you is just like the dynamics between any human beings. Some groups have a very rigid structure and offer many activities throughout the year. Other groups are casual, with a few activities, existing mostly to allow the children to play and be together in a safe and comfortable environment. You'll have to visit a few homeschooling groups to find out what you feel comfortable with. For instance, I have met very conservative religious mothers who attend secular groups that feel just right. I have also met mothers who are not religious, yet attend Christian groups because they like the structure and the organization such groups tend to have. Try many different groups, then stick with the one that feels best for you—or join more than one! Many families do.

Q My teenager wants to be homeschooled, but my husband and I both have to work. It doesn't seem like such a good idea. Does it ever work out?

A Of course, whether this will work or not depends on your teenager and the relationship you and your husband have with him or her. Some teenagers really appreciate being allowed to work on their own at home, having grown weary of their time being wasted in school or having to deal with negative peer pressure. They realize that concentrated work for three to four hours a day accomplishes all of their academic requirements and provides much more time for pursuing their own interests or getting a job. Keep in mind that only about two to three hours per day of classroom time is spent on academic pursuits, so that much time at home is usually more than adequate. Many teens also appreciate being treated as young adults rather than older children. Other teenagers fare better working a part-time job during the day and doing their academic work in the evening and on weekends.

Teenagers are at a perfect age to benefit from an apprentice situation or mentoring relationship, and homeschooled teenagers have the flexible time to take advantage of such an opportunity. We know of one teenager who works twenty-five hours a week in a pet store and plans on becoming a veterinarian. Another works part time at a newspaper office.

Q What will the neighbors think?

A Because homeschooling is not only legal in all states but also rapidly becoming more accepted as a mainstream way of life, this concern has decreased over the last ten years. But you may still face neighbors who are negative or even hostile to homeschooling. If possible, talk to them and quell their concerns. You can even send them a letter, explaining that homeschooling is legal, and so on, and letting them know that if they see your child playing outside during "school" hours, she is not truant. The bottom line is that homeschoolers no longer need to be afraid of recrimination from those with preconceived and uninformed notions.

Q Should I let my children play outside while regular school is in session?
   A Continuing the previous answer, as homeschooling is legal in every state, there's no reason to fear having your child playing on your block. If your children want to play at the park and are under adult supervision, most communities will not bother them. Get to know your community's attitude toward homeschoolers; if it is unfavorable, work to change it. In the late 1990s, some California communities tried to institute "curfew laws" that were successfully challenged in the courts when they were not enforced with good faith and common sense by police departments or truancy-control agencies. Be open and honest about homeschooling, and help local officials become more aware of homeschooling and its benefits to your community.

Q Is it harder to teach high school than the elementary grades?
   A Most people who homeschool high school–age students don't find any problem with teaching them. By this age, study habits have developed, and students are used to completing their schoolwork. In addition, students who have been in school and are now homeschooling typically enjoy finishing their schoolwork quickly, giving them time to work a part-time job, become an apprentice, participate in a sport, or take college classes.
   Parents of teenagers who have always been homeschooled may have to be more proactive in learning how to teach algebra, chemistry, or other more challenging subjects. Many families solve such problems by pooling their resources and hiring a tutor or teacher to instruct a small group (often five to ten children) in a particular subject, such as chemistry, once or twice a week. Usually this type of arrangement is conducive to a positive learning experience. The students are there for a specific reason, and they know that it is to their benefit to take advantage of such a class. With homeschooling becoming more popular each year, help is available to any family who wants it.

Q What if I can't stand to be with my kids all day?
   A In our experience, most of the types of children a parent wouldn't want to be around are not expressing their true personalities, but rather outward "faces" the children have created in response to marketing, school peer pressure, and the fear and low self-esteem that often

come with the school experience. This negative situation also breeds a feeling of alienation, and because parents are very often viewed by the schools as the enemy, children certainly don't feel comfortable turning to their parents for help.

Fortunately, people don't ask this question often, but when they do, we are always shocked and saddened. We believe parents who cannot stand to be with their children don't really know them, primarily due to the reasons just given. When your child is home with you, person-to-person, these negative external forces can—and do—fall away over time.

Children are people in their formative years; they should be guided and protected from what many adults today call "real" life—by which we mean exposure to social horrors (news coverage of mass deaths and heinous crime descriptions, leading to desensitization to violence) and the acceptance of personal "stylistic" trends, such as pierced body parts, tattoos, and the like. In our opinion, these aspects of "real" life are not necessary for happiness or harmony in *real* life and should be viewed as unnecessary by parents and children. Madison Avenue hucksterism and the pressure to blindly consume have helped dupe our American society into thinking that children are short adults with adult sensibilities—mature enough to make intelligent decisions about all they do and believe. A few minutes of close observation of an eleven-year-old or even a fifteen-year-old discloses the fallacy of this "short adult" assumption.

Children are capable of making *some* decisions, but in many others they need to be guided and steered. We all learn progressively how to navigate life—to make choices and determine what we believe and who we are. To become skilled at such decision making takes years. John Taylor Gatto, in his book *Dumbing Us Down,* comments that today's public school children never get the time alone required to build a personality but instead are constantly moved along the conveyor belt of scheduled activities or bombarded with media stimuli. Homeschooling provides the private time children need to build a personality. So it is not surprising that once your child has an opportunity to drop the facade that is reflecting Madison Avenue and the other kids at school and to return to his or her appropriate age and real self, chances are you will discover a pretty likeable person.

Q Should I get involved with the independent study program (ISP) with a public school?

A People who begin homeschooling often feel they need the warm hand of a certified teacher on their shoulder, guiding them along. After a year or two, some of them get the hang of doing it themselves and no longer need such guidance; others remain in the ISP for all of the child's school years. Providing such guidance is exactly what the public ISP appears to do. In most states, ISPs use the same curriculum that children at the local public school would use. If you choose such a program, you are assigned an ISP counselor—a certified teacher for the public school system, who usually keeps track of between one hundred and three hundred families just like yours. You are given the curriculum to follow and must report to the counselor weekly, bimonthly, or monthly, depending on the ISP's policy. Most families find, after a few months, that they love the freedom of homeschooling and want to be their own drivers.

Q I've never been a bookish person and did not like school. How can I possibly teach my children?

A Time and again, we hear from parents that homeschooling has afforded them the opportunity to educate or reeducate themselves in certain subjects. For example, you may not be interested in early history or word roots and grammar because of the negative feeling you have carried over from your own school days. But when reading about these to your child, you may find yourself becoming more interested as time goes on. If you take a positive approach, you can use homeschooling as an opportunity to learn new things of your own and add dimension to your life!

Q Homeschoolers seem to occupy the far left or the religious right, whereas I am somewhere in the middle. Where or how do I fit into all of this?

A Actually, political or religious orientation is as insignificant when it comes to teaching your children math as it is when teaching them how to tie their shoes. The perception has been that most homeschoolers did so for religious reasons, and that was truly the case for many years. But as more and more parents became dissatisfied with the academic weakness of public schools, yet often could not afford private schools, homeschooling's appeal broadened greatly, and now a large percentage of homeschooling's growth is in the "secular" part of society.

Since the late 1980s, homeschooling has become increasingly mainstream, attracting more and more professional or upper-income parents (along with lower- and middle-income families) opting to teach their own children at home—especially as the children approach high school age.

Q Don't teachers know something about "teaching" that we as parents should know to teach our own?

A No; as parents, we are already qualified to teach our own. The list of reasons why is long and different for each family. But you can begin with "I am my child's parent." Consider this: the schoolteacher's job is to present the curriculum chosen by the school administration to anywhere from twenty-five to forty children in a classroom setting, moving them through the school year on time. If the school board has decided that all fifth graders are going to be on page 165 of the math book by Thanksgiving, then the teacher's job is to make it so.

A homeschooling parent's job is very different. Just as you taught your children to eat with a fork and spoon, tie their shoes, make their bed, and so on you will be teaching them academic subjects. The same love and care that you used in teaching the nonacademic skills of life will carry over into the academic skills. You will be working with your children in a setting you choose (home) that you consider the right place for them. Unlike a classroom teacher, you can adjust your teaching focus at any time to meet the changing needs of your students and your family. Provided that your state doesn't require strict school year–type attendance records, you can work more during one part of the year, less during another. You can spend more time on an academic topic that a child is weak in and spend less time on a stronger academic topic.

Q If I have three children I want to homeschool, do I have to teach three levels of math, science, and English each day?

    A Probably not. One great thing about having two or more children in a homeschooling setting is that the younger ones want to keep up with the older ones. We are told that there is less total work when children are fairly close in age rather than farther apart. Some families report that their children set up a natural, healthy competition among themselves. In the case of English, the younger children may have to catch up to be on a par with the older, but will do that on their own. A few subjects will require individual, separate teaching, but probably only for a few minutes per day or week.

Q When will my child ever use calculus, trigonometry, algebra, or geometry?

    A Over the years, we have discussed this question with a number of math teachers. The consensus has been that unless the student intends to major in a math-intense subject such as architecture, engineering, astronomy, or computer programming, these higher forms of math are necessary only because colleges still require them for admissions. This seems to be a carryover from the early days of universities in the medieval period, but it doesn't seem particularly useful in the modern world. However, with all of the math help available in the form of in-person tutors, online tutors, DVD tutorials, and the like, it is not necessary for families who are homeschooling children in the early teen years to stress out about the higher math subjects. You can accomplish them before your student needs to have them completed in order to apply for college.

Q I enjoyed school activities like the prom and the science fair. Aren't we denying our children these things if we homeschool them?

    A If you feel that these activities are valuable additions to life, then you'll want to consider providing them for your children. However, keep in mind that homeschoolers tend to be very innovative. Many home-school groups have science fairs and social activities, sports teams and tournaments, and some provide eighth grade and high school gradu-ations for their students. Also, some homeschool groups arrange to participate with the local public school's science fairs and other such activities.

The beauty of something as grassroots as homeschooling is that you can make it anything you want it to be. Parents whose children are in the public school system often comment that they like a particular social activity—a dance, for instance—but they don't like the music being played. In homeschooling, we can create these activities for our chil-dren in an environment that is in harmony with our beliefs and values.

It would be unfair to mislead you that you can ensure these activities for your children without putting in work and effort. It takes all of the families in a homeschooling group to contribute to the grand scheme. If you are not the doer type, you can always join a private ISP, and the planning and prep will be done for you. Such groups usually cost any-where from $160 to $800 per year; they will advise you of the services they provide when you sign up. Be sure to ask, however; don't assume.

Q Are we losing a sense of community when we remove our children from school?

    A No. You are building a *true* sense of community when you decide to homeschool, if you also choose to meet with other homeschooling families and participate in the field trips, park days or play days, and any special programs they do. The mid-nineteenth-century, pre-Marxist-socialist, Utopian movement in America, which helped to create public schools, did so by trying to convince people that only through the government could a sense of community be built. This was contrary to all evidence that had gone before, particularly in the revolutionary and constitutional periods, in which the people them-selves voluntarily created and maintained very successful communities.

The same idea is still alive today: through programs like Goals 2000, the federal government, in our opinion, is trying to make public schools into synthetic "village centers." We think that it is better—and certainly more natural—for individual parents and families to create their own "villages." If you are used to having community activity planning done for you, you may have an adjustment to make. It is not difficult to do it yourself, however; the vast majority of homeschoolers have phones and cars and are on the Internet. You can communicate with them as easily as with someone in the PTA, Boy Scouts, or other community organization. It all comes down to this: you create and maintain the community—you don't expect homeschooling to do this for you.

Q   What about homeschooling an only child?

    A   As parents of an only child, we can answer, "We did it, and we think we were very successful." We know many other single-child families who have homeschooled, and they, too, have had great successes. We won't say it is easy; in fact, we believe it's harder to homeschool an only child. (Many of our homeschooling friends have two to eight children.) Much depends on the type of person your child is, as well. If she is incredibly social, it takes extra effort to plan a social life in which the child feels she interacts enough with other children. At least one parent must be the social type to plan a social life for the homeschooled child. Most homeschooling functions are not "drop-off" activities. If you are the parent caring for the child, you may find yourself spending hours on end with other homeschooling parents (mostly mothers). If you are not comfortable with this much socializing, it could be a problem for you.

    From an academic standpoint, homeschooling an only child can be tremendous fun. It is much easier to jump into the car and take off to the desert to see the wildflowers or to the ocean to explore tide pools with one child than with five or six children. One is also cheaper; you may be able to afford lessons that a large family might not be able to afford.

    Another advantage to homeschooling one child is the closeness that develops between the parents and the child. For us, spending day in and day out with our son gave us hours to talk and all get to know each other well. Mary has taken him along on many jobs to which she would not be able to take two or three children. She's even attended college classes with him right alongside her.

Q   Will my child have a high school diploma?

    A   Depending on your state's laws, probably yes—if you choose to obtain one. But check first. Generally speaking, your child can acquire a GED diploma through your state. Alternatively, if you have established your homeschool as your own certified private school, you as principal can create your own high school diploma. You may also use a nationally recognized, certified correspondence school to obtain a diploma. Check with the parent-run organization in your state (see Appendix A) to find out your state's requirements and guidelines.

Q How will I know if my child is "where she should be" in various subjects?

    A You can always give her a standardized test. There are many private companies that offer these tests and will grade them as well (see Part Four, Homeschooling Resources).

However, if you want a real-life answer to this question, we can offer this one: when our son was about eleven, he developed a concern about what grade he was in, as many of the school children he met in his choir rehearsals would start a conversation by asking that question. We had used a boxed curriculum for fourth grade, but then began following our own ideas about what he needed to learn and when. At age eleven, his reading comprehension and pronunciation were at college level, he was doing fifth-grade math, and his handwriting was equal to that of many adults—certainly more legible than the writing of most children his age. We explained to him that we weren't "doing" grade levels, but following a different path; therefore, he knew different levels of different subjects. This answer resolved his concerns and he understood his "grade" position clearly thereafter.

The point is, when it comes to determining where a child should be academically, there is a great deal more latitude than the public school mind-set would have you think. The administrations or school boards set standards, but these may often be arbitrary. In America in the 1800s, a fifth-grade student may well have been doing work that we would assign to college freshmen today. Certainly, many of the Founding Fathers were much more knowledgeable and intellectually advanced than their counterparts today seem to be!

Realizing that this idea of standards is fairly arbitrary, a parent can begin to see that homeschooling affords students the opportunity to soar ahead in favored topics of study and still spend plenty of time on their less-popular academic areas. Keep in mind that most classrooms use a grading curve or similar arbitrary measurement of performance. Any adult who remembers "cramming" for an exam and then trying to recall the crammed information two weeks later knows that the grade achieved on the test was not a reflection of what she actually knew about the subject, but was the result of applied short-term memory. What your homeschooled child actually knows is more apparent through day-to-day observation than by any other form of assessment.

Q   Should I use a prepackaged curriculum?

A   If you are new to homeschooling and don't know where to begin, then a prepackaged curriculum could be ideal for you and your child. Prepackaged curricula give beginning homeschooling parents a direction—even seasoned homeschoolers often continue to use a prepackaged curriculum. If they do not hinder your sense of freedom from school, they are a wonderful way to go. Our advice is to try one for a grade and don't be reluctant to reshape it to suit your child's specific needs.

Q   What about college?

A   All major colleges and universities accept homeschoolers, with a few exceptions. When you begin the college admissions process, check with each school on its policies and requirements about homeschoolers, since they can and do change from time to time. Admissions offices can generally spot good prospects, and the homeschooled child with a high enough SAT score who does well in an interview will be welcomed. Some institutions of higher learning even seek out homeschoolers! This is because homeschooling *tends* to produce children who do not embark on an academic path unless they are serious about its completion. This isn't to say that no homeschooler ever dropped a college class or failed one—or dropped out of college altogether. But once you begin to homeschool and you and your children take academics seriously as an important and valuable part of life—not some mandatory time that has to be put in, as it is too commonly in school—that seriousness becomes part of your children's makeup. They will likely not enjoy *wasting* time on academics, but will want to get the work done so that other things can be pursued—just as the typical fifth- or sixth-grade homeschooler does.

Q   How do homeschooled children "turn out" as adults?

A   There are a number of books and even a documentary movie chronicling adult homeschooled children. Basically they are just like any other young adults. They hold a variety of jobs, attend virtually any college or university, marry, have children of their own, and so on. Of course, if they have grown up without the "cultural" influence of mainstream society, they may be a bit more relaxed and comfortable with themselves than their public school counterparts. They may be a little more self-assured because they have not been made to feel inadequate by constant testing and comparison with others. But of course, the public school system also produces similarly confident individuals, so homeschooled adults don't glaringly stand out in any way.

Q Is there a downside to homeschooling?

A Challenges such as a family's living on one income, learning how to be together day in and day out, and the adults' having to relearn or learn certain academic subjects, at first may seem like negatives, but if you give yourself the opportunity to discover that these negatives can be positives, homeschooling can lead to the greatest metamorphosis of your life! Speaking of our own experience, we are satisfied with our decision to homeschool, and there has not been a downside that we consider worthy of mention. What at first seemed like adversity has grown into a new, freer, and much larger life than we originally dreamed of.

Take-Away Points

- Your child will probably teach you that you should be proud to be homeschoolers.
- You will get to know your child's true self—not the one that she has created as a survival or defense mechanism for school use.
- Some teenagers seem relieved to be taken out of a peer-dependent environment.
- Your child is the best example of the fruits of homeschooling.
- Most people who homeschool high schoolers don't find teaching them a problem. Teaching higher-level math is not difficult with all of the help (CDs, tutors, and so on) available.
- Use homeschooling as an opportunity to learn new things and add dimension to your life.
- Homeschooling can lead to the greatest metamorphosis of your life!

List 1.5. Glossary of Common Homeschooling Terms

The following are terms and organizational names that the new homeschooling parent is likely to hear often in conversations or discussions about homeschooling. It will help you in the early stages to familiarize yourself with some of them.

Accreditation.   Certification of a school by an accrediting board that inspects it and, on approval, provides it with a certificate of approval or a certificate of accreditation.

Auditory learner.   One who learns best by hearing information rather than by seeing it written down.

Charlotte Mason approach. Method of homeschooling founded by Charlotte Mason, a teacher in Victorian England who advocated educating children by offering them a gentle, full life with daily observation of nature, exposure to music, and the use of living books (as opposed to textbooks that do not allow the characters to come to life), and other high-quality activities.

Charter school.   There are two categories of charter schools—those that operate as independent wings of an existing public school and those that are privately owned and operated. The public charter school typically is a section of the bricks-and-mortar school, where homeschooling parents and their students meet with an assigned teacher to receive guidance and receive curriculum materials. The school receives the Average Daily Attendance (ADA) funds for the student, just as if he were in school. The school district determines how much autonomy parents will have.

The privately owned charter school has to adhere to certain state-imposed terms of the charter, but usually has a bit more flexibility than public charter schools.

Child-led learning.   An approach in homeschooling in which the child's needs and interests are considered first and foremost, and the parents take their cue from the child, as opposed to requiring the child to simply conform to the parents' ideas of what the child should learn.

Classical education.   Also known as the trivium or "three roads." The three roads are grammar, logic, and rhetoric. Together with the quadrivium or "four roads"—arithmetic, geometry, music, and astronomy—they make up the liberal arts. These seven subjects formed the curriculum of the medieval university in Europe. The classical education method is very popular among certain homeschoolers, who often have their children learn the classical languages, Latin or Greek, as well.

Correspondence school. The traditional distance-learning mode that provides long-distance educational services, giving students the option of mailing in assignments that are then graded by a staff teacher and returned. Many colleges and universities are adding Internet-based delivery of instruction, assignments, and grading to their distance-learning departments.

Curriculum. Course of study, homeschooling or otherwise. It may be composed of textbooks, workbooks, and other prepackaged materials or may be completely made up from scratch, to fit parents' objectives.

Decompression. In the homeschooling context, the act of a child's releasing the negative pressure built up from a school setting once the child begins homeschooling.

Delayed academics. The philosophy that young children should not be pressured with instruction in the "academic subjects" (such as reading, writing, and math), but should be allowed to mature into their skills at their own individual rates. This philosophy was brought to light by the late Dr. Raymond and Dorothy Moore, as a result of their pioneering work in studying childhood development.

Eclectic approach. Method of homeschooling that uses materials from any and all sources, rather than following a preset program or curriculum.

Goals 2000. Federal government program that sought to make each public school into a sort of village center for dispensing and monitoring a wide variety of medical, social, and family programs. The wording of its provisions was mandatory, not voluntary, and it was viewed by its critics as a further encroachment on personal and family freedom for those families within the public school system. Although the name will have changed, there is no doubt among watchdog groups that at some level of the federal government the ideology of Goals 2000 lives on and may rise again. Therefore, it is important for homeschoolers to remain aware of it.

Growing Without Schooling. No longer in print, *GWS* was a bimonthly published by John Holt from the 1970s to 2003. Along with the *Moore Report,* *GWS* was one of the first publications devoted to *unschooling.* Therefore, it led the way in the modern homeschooling movement. See *Unschooling method.*

Holt Associates. Company that sponsors a yearly conference in Massachusetts and publishes many homeschooling books. Headed by Pat Farenga.

Homeschool Legal Defense Association (HSLDA). An advocacy organization cofounded by homeschooling dad and attorney Mike Farris. HSLDA offers homeschooling legal advice and representation to its subscriber members.

Independent study program (ISP). A program offered by public schools and private organizations through which you can homeschool your children using the same curriculum and schedule offered in the day school. Because states have different designations for this facility, please check yours.

Kinesthetic learner.   One who learns best by feeling or touching; also called a *tactile learner.*

Language arts.   The study of the English language, reading, spelling, grammar, and literature.

Learning styles.   Three learning styles—visual, auditory, and kinesthetic or tactile—that were discovered in the late twentieth century by researchers on child learning. For each of us, one of these styles dominates, meaning we take in information and learn best in that manner, although we make use of the other two styles as well.

Moore Formula.   Philosophy developed by the late Dr. Raymond and Dorothy Moore, which says that work and service along with study from books provide a balanced education. The formula also advocates not forcing academics until the child is mature and ready to receive them.

Moore Foundation.   Serves homeschool families with educational material that supports the Moore Formula. Can also be used as a correspondence school.

Park day.   A common term used for the social-mixing day that homeschoolers all around the United States experience. In most places "park day" can also mean a get-together at someone's house; it does not have to be at a park.

Phonics.   A method of teaching the acts of reading, spelling, and pronunciation by using the phonetic sounds of letters. The approach opposite to phonics is *whole language.*

Principle approach.   Method of homeschooling based on Biblical principles.

Scope and Sequence.   The time line for completing the work for a particular book or program. For instance, if you have a textbook that provides a Scope and Sequence, it will advise you to have finished Chapter 51 by Thanksgiving, or Section 5 by twelve weeks into the work, or some other measure of work to be accomplished by a certain time. It is meant to provide a guideline for how quickly the student should progress on average. This term is used often in school settings, but homeschooling products refer to it as well.

Socialization.   Process of shaping and molding behavior and interaction within a certain social group or stratum. Everyone is "socialized" either positively or negatively.

Summerhill.   Experimental boarding school in Suffolk England, founded by the late A. S. Neill in 1921, that originally took "problem" students and offered them a completely noncompulsory atmosphere in which to learn. Classes were held, but no student was required to attend. The underlying theory is that when a student has his interest in some field of endeavor or study piqued, he will then develop the desire to nurture that interest. For example, if a boy realizes that he dreams of building buildings and houses, he will summon the will to do well in math to make this dream come true. Summerhill is still operating, and accepting students. See www.summerhillschool.co.uk for information.

Tactile learner.   One who learns best by touching; also called a *kinesthetic learner.*

Trivium approach.   See *Classical education.*

Umbrella school.   School or church that functions as a legal cover for homeschoolers in some states.

Unit study.   Method of study in which an entire program with a unifying theme is created to study diverse topics.

Unschooling method.   Method of homeschooling in which learning is led by the child's interests primarily, rather than by a predetermined curriculum or the parents' desires.

Visual learner.   One who learns best by seeing, as opposed to hearing.

Voucher.   In the schooling sense, a credit given by the government for taxpayers to use for their choice of private, public, or correspondence school.

Whole language.   Method of teaching reading or other subjects that advocates having experiences and memorizing words to develop a total experience that is then blended together, enabling students to learn the material in a more "whole" approach. The approach opposite to whole language is *phonics.*

Part Two

Homeschooling Models and Methods

Homeschooling is, at first glance, a simple proposition: the parent or guardian teaches the child at home, either autonomously or under the direction of a teacher. For those parents who work under the direction of a teacher, there may not be very much freedom in what materials are used or what approach is taken.

However, for the autonomous parent, who is teaching on his or her own authority, there are a number of methods or approaches for imparting knowledge to the child that bear discussing and consideration. Each one has its strength and its weakness, its attractiveness and its drawback. For the seven described here, we will provide enough of an overview that you can investigate further and develop your own point of view. We offer the general list and then focus on each method and the resources available for it.

List 2.1. Methods of Homeschooling

- The Charlotte Mason approach
- The trivium approach
- The unschooling approach
- Eclectic homeschooling
- The delayed academic method
- The unit study approach
- The principle approach

List 2.2. The Charlotte Mason Method

Charlotte Mason (1842–1923) was born in England and worked as a teacher. She was homeschooled herself, and as an adult she composed *Home Education*, a six-volume set (called the Original volumes or series) putting forth her beliefs and ideas, which is still available. Ms. Mason's basic philosophy was that above all, children should love to learn, and teaching should aid and nurture such love, not restrict and limit it. She believed in providing "living" books, in which the characters come to life as real people, as opposed to textbooks, in which the information is generally dry and lifeless. Charlotte Mason continues to influence homeschoolers, and her method has fostered many websites and blogsites, producing and supporting many different products and services. Here are some of the best:

- *Books by Catherine Levison.* Ms. Levison lives in Washington state and has homeschooled her five children for over ten years using the tenets of Charlotte Mason. She began by applying one small aspect at a time, after the regular homeschooling work for the week had been finished. Ms. Levison has written a considerable number of books on the Mason method, including two concise "how-to" manuals, *A Charlotte Mason Education* and its sequel, *More Charlotte Mason Education.* PMB 500, 2522 N. Proctor, Tacoma, WA 98406; 253-879-0433.
- *Charlotte Mason Research and Supply Company.* Founded and owned by Karen Andreola. Ms. Andreola began applying the CM techniques over ten years ago and found that some were easier for her family to accommodate than others, but gradually they have incorporated all of them, to their benefit. They operate the CMR&SC, and Karen writes books as well. Her *Charlotte Mason Companion* is very popular and useful to those interested in or already using the CM approach. P.O. Box 296, Quarryville, PA 17566; http://www.charlottemason.com.
- *Queen Homeschool Supply.* "Publishers of books for the Charlotte Mason style educator." This website provides extensive products and resources for the CM homeschooler. Book titles cover over twenty-four topics and provide learning materials for the CM family, whatever their need may be. There are titles dealing with courtship, character building, and preparation for marriage, as well as the regular academic topics, such as geography materials, language arts, history, and so on.

   Many of these titles are originals by Sandi Queen or others, so this website is a must-see for CM parents. 168 Plantz Ridge Road, New Freeport, PA 15352; 888-695-2777; www.queenhomeschool.com.
- *Books and products by Penny Gardner.* Ms. Gardner is the author of *The Charlotte Mason Study Guide: A Simplified Approach to Family Living,*

as well as a handwriting book and a nine-note recorder. She is a home-schooling mom of six children and an enthusiastic fan of CM methods and practices. Her website has many, many resources for CM families. www.pennygardner.com.

- *A Charlotte Mason Education.* This is a very complete website maintained by Deborah Taylor-Hough, a well-known homeschooling author and lecturer on many topics. Her CM site includes writings from Catherine Levison and a guide on how to read the six volumes of Mason's Original series. http://sites.silaspartners.com/cmason.

- *Simply Charlotte Mason.com.* This site offers many resources and ideas; registration required. P.O. Box 892, Grayson, GA 30017; www.simplycharlottemason.com.

- *Living Literature.* Although this site has not been updated in a number of years, its value has not diminished with time. If you view it as an old library of articles about the CM method, from diverse modern sources and discussing a myriad of topics, it will serve you well. http://home. att.net/~d.hiffernan/charlottemason.html.

- *Ambleside Online.* Ambleside Online (AO) is a curriculum guide, book-list, and other resources, designed to follow Charlotte Mason's method of homeschooling. There is a list of books provided by grade or study year that will apply to that year. The curriculum is provided in order to free parents from the task of having to create a curriculum from scratch so they can find the time to teach it as well. AO takes the guesswork out of the curriculum part. AO makes it clear that these books do not have to be purchased; many are available at libraries, and the family can substitute its own books instead. AO also notes that families use as much or as little of the suggestions as they like. Some follow the curriculum guide exactly; most take bits and pieces of its advice, even down to simply using just the Picture Study, the Composer Study, and the like. AO points out that the curriculum alone will not provide your child with a CM education; that requires that you understand Mason's vision and philosophy, and that you teach your children yourself every day. The website provides the Original volumes to read online in both the original Victorian English version and a modern version; it also offers an online study group for parents, so they don't have to read the Original volumes alone! Ambleside Online is completely free of charge and provides very extensive information. www.amblesideonline.org.

- *Website by Lynn B Hocraffer.* This site offers Study Notes from Lynn's discussion groups and contains many interesting items, including Notes on CM for High School Ages. http://homepage.bushnell.net/ ~peanuts/CMason.html.

- *A Charlotte Mason Study Loop.* This study loop relating to the CM approach is moderated by three different women, who offer a great deal of information and advice about the CM world. http://www.angelfire.com/journal/CharlotteMason/.
- *A Catholic Charlotte Mason site.* The site advises that non-Catholics are welcome, but that it keeps true to the tenets of Catholicism. http://www.4reallearning.com.
- *Another Catholic CM site.* Besides valuable homeschooling resources and essays, this site contains articles by two grown students who attended PNEU schools in England, providing a firsthand glimpse into the ultimate results of Ms. Mason's methods. http://www.materamabilis.org/.
- *Nancy "Macbeth" CM site.* A woman named Nancy (aka Macbeth), who homeschools her four children, offers this site, wherein she too provides a vast array of CM information and links to even more! This is a great resource for the entire family and is very entertaining for anyone wishing to learn and use the Charlotte Mason way. http://charlottemason.tripod.com/.
- *A California Latter Day Saints Charlotte Mason website.* This site also provides support group information for California LDS members and an extensive list of virtual field trips and other activities. http://ldshomeschoolinginca.org/cm.html.

List 2.3. Classical Education – The Trivium

In the modern context, the oldest method of "homeschooling" in the Western world is what is commonly known as classical education or the trivium, which means "three roads." The three roads are grammar, logic, and rhetoric. Together with the quadrivium or "four roads," arithmetic, geometry, music and astronomy, these seven subjects—the liberal arts—formed the curriculum of the medieval university in Europe. These topics of study had been followed in the classical world; European scholars saw their value in developing and cultivating a human mind—as opposed to letting it grow "wild."

Many homeschooling families favor the classical education approach and include it as their curriculum, as it teaches many important skills:

- *Grammar* covers language skills; that is, reading and creative writing. The goal of teaching grammar is to provide your student with a large enough vocabulary and mechanical knowledge of how to use it, so that when she actually has something to write, she won't be tripped up on simple issues of "how to."
- Through *logic*—the practice and method of thought—the student learns how to analyze and think critically, rather than simply form opinions. It also requires the student to recognize the difference between a theory and a proven fact. The original scientific method was based on this discipline.
- *Rhetoric* provides the student with the ability to persuade others and make a logical case for his thoughts—rather than to simply form opinions that are not based on thought.

A primary goal of the classical method of homeschooling is to teach the child how to learn and teach himself or herself throughout life. Parents give the child the tools to learn and, later, the information to be learned.

In the past ten years, the resources available for the classical method have exploded, facilitated by the proliferation of the Internet.

Classical education often included the study of Latin and Greek, so that students could read the classics of Western thought in the original languages. For instance, the popular British author C. S. Lewis was taught in this way. Modern homeschoolers often follow this practice, too.

The *ultimate* goal of using the classical method in modern times is to make sure that your child grows up being able to think independently and clearly on any topic, as well as knowing what great thinking has gone before us and contributed to the building of Western civilization.

The following are some of the best classical homeschooling resources:

- *Memoria Press.* This publisher of classical ed materials also produces a quarterly magazine, *The Classical Teacher,* published by Cheryl Lowe and edited by Martin Cothran. Ms. Lowe has written extensively about the classical method, and you can read many of her excellent pieces on the Memoria Press website. The entire site is brimming over with great thought and encouragement, even if you wish to provide your child with only a smattering of the skills developed in the classical method. 4105 Bishop Lane, Louisville, KY 40218; 877-862-1097 or 502-966-9115; magister@memoriapress.com; http://www.memoriapress.com.
- *Escondido Tutorial Service (ETS).* ETS is a very thorough and valuable Christian classical resource. The site contains interesting links to other equally valuable sites, which will also be mentioned later. ETS also provides background explanations of why to use the classical approach and an excellent list of books and materials to purchase for further information on the classical method. Email: gbt@gbt.org; http://www.gbt.org.
- *The Well-Trained Mind* (Norton, 1999), by Susan Wise-Bauer and Jessie Wise, and *The Well-Educated Mind* (Norton, 2004), by Susan Wise-Bauer, are two books that have become modern pillars of thought and practice for the classical method in homeschooling. Susan, Jessie's daughter, is a grown-up homeschooler, a professor of English at William & Mary College, and a homeschooling mom herself. She has written extensively about the classical approach, and her books and speeches on the topic inspire many parents. Visit her website for much more information. www.susanwisebauer.com.
- *Classical Homeschooling Magazine.* This well-fashioned publication is "[d]evoted exclusively to promoting and reporting on the growing revival of Classical Education for homeschooling parents, homeschooling students, Classical Charter and Private Schools' Great Books Readers." There are four issues offered completely online, brimming with information and knowledge. P.O. Box 10726, Bainbridge Island, WA 98110; http://www.classicalhomeschooling.com.
- *Trivium Pursuit.* This company, founded and run by the Bluedorn family of Illinois, all 100 percent Christian homeschoolers, is the main source for a wide variety of books and other trivium teaching materials. It is a Christian company founded and operated by the homeschooling family of Harvey and Laurie Bluedorn and their five children. Harvey and Laurie have also written a useful book

gleaned from their experiences of homeschooling since the early 1980s, called *Teaching the Trivium*. http://www.triviumpursuit.com. Their two oldest sons, Nathan and Hans, have their own websites—http://www.bloomingthorn.com and http://www.christianlogic.com, respectively—where they post their writings relating to logic and reasoning, especially as it relates to the modern world and media. These sites provide excellent information and guidance to anyone interested in the trivium.

- *Trivium.net.* This interesting Australian website has much detailed information regarding the trivium and is worth the time spent reading over it, even if you don't use the trivium. However, it does not provide specific resources for materials or guidance. If you already using the classical approach, it can provide you with general information. http://www.trivium.net/.

List 2.4. Classical Education Colleges

There are three prominent colleges that use the classical approach. There may be many more smaller ones opening all the time, but two of these have been around for many years.

- *Thomas Aquinas College.* Aquinas College is a four-year Catholic liberal arts college located in Santa Paula, approximately sixty-five miles northwest of Los Angeles. Aquinas uses the tutorial method, just as Oxford and Cambridge do, and is based upon the classical approach. The "Great Books"—such as the writings of St. Augustine, Aristotle, Plato, and of course, St. Thomas Aquinas—are studied and discussed in an atmosphere of friendly but intense academic exploration. The students discuss and debate with each other, tossing ideas back and forth; the instructor generally acts as a moderator and guide during these sessions. It is not necessary to have been taught by the classical method prior to entrance, nor is it necessary to be Catholic to attend TAC, but chapel attendance is mandatory. 10000 N. Ojai Road, Santa Paula, CA 93060; 800-634-9797 or 805-525-4417.
- *St. John's College.* Both campuses of the three-hundred-year-old St. John's College—in Santa Fe, New Mexico, and Annapolis, Maryland—provide the same attractive classical approach to earning a bachelor's degree in liberal arts. The classroom discussions are similar to those described for Thomas Aquinas College, with the instructor acting as moderator and guide while the students "teach themselves" via the Great Books. All incoming freshman learn the same things at the same time, progressing through all four years on an equal footing. There are lectures only once a week; the rest of the time is devoted to reading assignments, participating in discussion, and writing papers. Students can transfer between the two campuses during their four years, but no outside transfers are allowed, as there are no electives in the program. All freshmen study the same subjects at the same time, and continue to do so throughout their four years at St. John's. St John's has no religious affiliation. It also does not rely on the SAT scores, but rather on its own essay questions and live interviews with prospective freshmen. 1160 Camino Cruz Blanca, Santa Fe, NM 87505-4599; 505-984-6000 or 60 College Avenue, Annapolis, MD 21401; 410-263-2371; http://www.sjcsf.edu/.
- *Patrick Henry College (PHC).* PHC is a relatively new school, having begun operation in September 2000, and it is dedicated to Christian teaching. In the first two years, students follow a course of study familiar to all in the classical method—logic and rhetoric, followed by theology, philosophy, history, constitutional law, language, literature,

economics, mathematics, science, and more. Then, in the last two years, the student chooses to major in either government or classical liberal arts, applying the knowledge and skill developed in the first two years to practical professional training in their field. P.O. Box 1776, Purcellville, VA 20134-1776; ph. 540-338-1776, fax 540-338-8707; info@phc.edu.

List 2.5. The Unschooling Method

In the late 1960s, the late Boston educator John C. Holt came up with some ideas about learning that startled many of his colleagues and formed the basis of the unschooling movement in homeschooling. After formulating his basic theories that children are naturally curious and will lead themselves in exploring and finding out about the world around them, Holt worked to bring about school reform, attempting to implement his ideas in the classroom setting to which he was accustomed.

Unschooling means "Don't do as schools do": stifling the child's natural learning impulses, forcing intellectual activity to be subject to a rigid timetable, and so on.

Today, many parents have interpreted unschooling as meaning "Don't do anything academic unless your child initiates the interest." Despite such assumptions, unschooling is not a complete negation of academics. If children want to study chemistry, you can still teach them as unschoolers—maybe by doing chemistry all day and forgoing anything not required for the study of chemistry. A child may need to learn to print in order to copy formulas or take notes, so the child will eagerly learn to print well to further his or her chemistry exploration. This would be *the* definition of unschooling: "Forget what the school agenda is; teach chemistry."

Many unschooling parents are striving to preserve the ideal of the self-motivated child—one who is constantly exploring and discovering relevant information, hands-on, not just in books. The information that children learn becomes integrated into their personalities—possibly for life. To unschoolers, gardening is just as important as math, building a soapbox racer is equal in importance to reading, and watching baby kittens being born is on a par with (if not superior to) knowing the definitions of nouns and verbs at a prescribed point in life.

Here are some of the best unschooling resources:

- *Unschooling.org.* This site, also called the Family Unschoolers Network (FUN), provides links to other unschooling resources and is the site for the John Holt Bookstore, having taken over the book sales duties from Holt Associates a number of years ago. It has an interesting book catalogue, especially of valuable out-of-print books worth considering.
- *www.unschooling.com.* This website provides general information about unschooling as well as links to some other unschooling resources. It also provides whatever back issues are extant of *Growing Without Schooling,* Holt's seminal homeschooling publication. Holt's writings and dialogue with readers of *GWS* are inspiring and worth reading again and again.

List 2.6. The Eclectic Style

The eclectic style of homeschooling makes use of the vast resources available to those who are interested in knowing more. Everywhere you go, there are things to know and learn. In the homeschooling realm, the eclectic style draws from the other methods or approaches in order to teach more fully. Those who follow this style are willing to choose materials from diverse sources; they view each child as an individual who responds to methods and materials differently from how, for example, a sibling responds to it.

An eclectic homeschooling parent might choose to teach grammar, logic, and rhetoric (the trivium) because it develops in a child the ability to reason, form intelligent concepts, and analyze the thoughts of others. That same family may teach basic science by gardening and the ancillary activities that accompany it. They may teach math by food shopping and cooking, or running a household, which requires budgeting and later analysis.

In the realm of book choices, the family following an eclectic approach might use a math book from the early twentieth century, found at a used bookstore for $1, for one child, but a math book recently published for another child. They combine that with a spelling book from the 1950s, also found at the same used bookstore, but they also use an almost-new modern history book and a brand-new political geography book because these subjects change over time. Language arts, math, and ancient history all remain the same, but modern history and the boundaries of countries and their social implications are ever-evolving.

The idea of being an eclectic homeschooling family is not so much a philosophy as a comfort level of being able to pick and choose as one wishes and according to what one sees as significant. It is likely that many teachers who choose to homeschool their children are in this category, as they have the self-confidence to pick up a book out of a pile and know within a few moments if it is of value to them or not.

Many parents are intimidated by the prospect of being teachers; they feel they don't know how to do it or where to begin. But most public school teachers don't choose their curriculum either, although they are trained to. Unfortunately, it is chosen for them by the administration, and they are required to present that material to their students.

To allay the fears of the beginning homeschooling family, publishers offer many potentially helpful products and resources that come with teacher's manuals. This is one reason why homeschooling parents are able to say (without smugness or judgment of the trained teacher) that teaching your own children does not require special ability or intelligence, just the desire to do so and the ability to read and then impart the information. Most parents soon realize that they can teach their own children up to at least the high school level. There is no end to the help available to those who seek it.

Here are some of the best eclectic resources:

- *EHO – Eclectic Homeschooling Online.* This website offers a great starting place for those who wish to know about the eclectic approach, or those who already know and want to find resources and connect with other like-minded families. http://eclectichomeschool.org/store/.
- *Homeschool Mom.* This site offers a wide variety of articles and links by such notable authors as Cafi Cohen, Terri McKee, and Beverly Krueger. It also provides free resources—a sure-fire hit with eclectics. www.thehomeschoolmom.com.
- *Homeschool.com's Eclectic Kit.* This kit contains a wealth of products for the eclectic homeschooling family, including a four-CD set of live presentations by Diane Flynn Keith, Beverly Krueger, Pat Wyman, and Valerie Bendt. It will provide answers to virtually any question one might have about this approach to homeschooling. www.homeschool.com/eclectic.
- *The Homeschool Zone.* The "Zone" contains a wealth of resources for anyone interested in homeschooling. It has links to important books about homeschooling along with how to start a support group, recipes, and lots of other great items. www.homeschoolzone.com.

List 2.7. The Delayed Academic Approach

The delayed academic approach was created by the late Dr. Raymond and Dorothy Moore. They partially homeschooled their two children as pioneers in the homeschooling movement of the 1980s and were responsible for the passage of many homeschooling laws in California. They began their activities in the homeschooling movement at the same time as their friend John Holt.

Delayed academics means that, for instance, if a child does not learn to read until sometime between eight and twelve years old, this is not a cause for anxiety. The Moores demonstrated that children who learn to read at this "delayed" time do not suffer for it and within a year or two are on par with children who learn to read at a much younger age—possibly when they were not ready to do so.

Raymond Moore was known worldwide for establishing highly successful work-study programs in colleges and universities. Dorothy was a child specialist and reading and curriculum authority. Their methods have been used by thousands of families, schools, and homeschools around the world that want to develop high achievement, social ability, and character in their students and children.

Three Steps for the Delayed Approach

The delayed academic approach involves following the Moore formula (as quoted from a Moore Foundation manual): "1. Study every day, from a few minutes to hours. 2. Manual work, at least as much as study. 3. Home and/or community service, an hour or so per day. Focus on kids' interests and needs; be an example in consistency, curiosity and patience. Live with them! Worry less about tests. With the Moore formula, if you are loving and can read, write, count and speak clearly, you are a master teacher."

Thousands of Studies Bear Out the Delayed Approach

The Moore Foundation has conducted thousands of studies and paired them with studies from Stanford University and the University of Colorado Medical School. They concluded, after observing children's senses, brain, cognition, and so on, that no evidence shows that children are ready for or need formal study or homeschool before the ages of eight to ten. The Moores' method advocates, rather than trying to conduct classroom-type instruction for younger children, simply reading aloud to your children as well as singing and playing with them from birth. They suggest that children will learn to read in their own time, if someone reads to them often. Some children are not actually ready until the age of fourteen! Dr. Moore claimed that the older learners often become the best readers of all. They also experience less damaged vision, more adult-like reasoning, more mature brain structure, and less blocking of creative interests.

Not the Same as Unschooling

The delayed approach is not an unschooling program; it is placing service and work interests before "bookish" academics. The Moores point out that most of us learn what we *do*, not what is stuffed into our heads!

Here are some of the best delayed academics resources:

- *The Moore Foundation, Academy and Bookstore.* Of course, this is *the* source for information about the Moores' approach to home-schooling. They belonged to the Seventh-Day Adventist branch of Christianity, and much of their philosophy was focused on community service and character building. Their academy offers guidance counseling, the complete study program, and a way to impart information to the younger child that makes it possible for parents who use the Moore Academy to satisfy the early education laws in their state without damaging the child in the process with too much formal education. Please see the site for much valuable information. P.O. Box 98, N. Bonneville, WA 98639; 509-427-7779; www.moorefoundation.com.
- *Key Curriculum Press.* The Key website offers many delayed-academic approved products, and others, including curriculum choices and unusual software like Tinkerplots and the Geometer's Sketchpad. www.keypress.com.
- *TOPS Science.* TOPS offers original science material and information, including inexpensive projects that can be made from household ingredients. They also provide some free, downloadable materials. Their website is worth spending some time with. www.topscience.com.
- *Archers for the Lord (formerly The Relaxed Christian Homeschooler).* This is the website and organization of Dr. Mary Hood, a very well known and popular relaxed Christian homeschooler, which in some cases has been interpreted as unschooling. Because of the confusion about the term *unschooler*—which many people interpret as undisciplined, untrained children running amok—Dr. Hood emphasizes that homeschooling is first about home and second about school. This places her position in perspective very quickly and clearly. P.O. Box 2524, Cartersville, GA 30120; maryhood@archersforthelord.org; www.archersforthelord.com.

List 2.8. The Unit Study Approach

Unit study is a holistic approach, focusing all subjects on one central theme. Unit study involves taking a particular topic—such as ancient Rome—and studying it for a month or longer, using it as the theme for learning all other subjects. During your study of Rome, you can incorporate different academics—by using Roman games, coin values, numerals, literature, history, and even Latin—to gain insight into the Roman world and learn math, history, geography, art, spelling, writing—all in one holistic package. You can also cook and eat Roman food, go to a museum to see Roman artwork, read history about Julius Caesar or the great orator Cicero, or read the poetry of Virgil (you get the picture!).

Flexibility

Besides providing a meaningful anchor to your child's learning experience, another unique aspect of unit study is that you can do it from an unschooling approach, by allowing your child to choose what to study. If you unit-study astronomy and your child is more interested in the planets than the constellations, you can concentrate on that aspect. Unit study is very flexible, yet effective. It represents total immersion, just like the most powerful foreign language learning programs.

Write Your Own or Buy a Prepared Unit Study

If you are a particularly imaginative and motivated parent, you can come up with your own unit study syllabus, or you can purchase one that is already prepared for you. You can even take unit study to the extreme of visiting a foreign country you have studied—or decide to use a country you are going to visit as the basis for your unit study.

Here are some of the best unit study resources:

- *www.unitstudy.com.* Amanda Bennett, author of the book *Unit Study 101,* owns this very useful and helpful website, which provides insights into why and how she turned to the unit study approach. She provides ready-to-use unit studies for sale here, and her book is available on CD-ROM, too, so you can purchase it and print it as you need each section.
- *Cadron Creek Publishing.* Cadron Creek is a Christian company that provides many prepared and interesting unit studies, including *Little House on the Prairie* (pioneer era), C. S. Lewis's *The Chronicles of Narnia,* and *Anne of Green Gables* (Victorian era), as well as other excellent study materials and ideas. They also offer two CD-ROMs of music

from the *Little House* series! One is fiddle tunes from that era and place; the other contains eighteen songs that "Pa" Ingalls sang, as referenced in the books. Cadron Creek Christian Curriculum, 4329 Pinos Altos Rd., Silver City, NM 88061; 505-534-1496; www.cadroncreek.com.

- *Homefires.* This website is owned and moderated by Diane Flynn Keith, one of the most knowledgeable and communicative people in homeschooling. She offers a huge amount of information for all homeschoolers, but in the unit study area she has a particularly useful virtual conference: a Q and A section with Tina Fermin, Shannon Hawkins, and Delaine Noyer, three experienced homeschooling moms who offer excellent day-to-day advice. www.homefires.com.

- *Konos (Christian).* Konos is one of the oldest unit study publishers in homeschooling, and a family-owned business to boot! They provide complete resources to Christian families who desire a Bible-based point of view with quality materials. Please see their website for detailed information. KONOS, Inc., P.O. Box 250, Anna, TX 75409; ph.: 972-924-2712; info@konos.com; www.konos.com.

- *Five in a Row (Christian).* This very-well-known unit study program was created by Jane Claire Lambert, a homeschooling mom of seventeen years' experience. Its three volumes contain fifty-five lesson plans, based on outstanding books, and the course teaches social studies, language arts, math, and science. Each day's work is laid out clearly, and the website claims that it takes only five minutes of teacher preparation each day. Ms. Lambert has also developed a complete series of products based on the Five in a Row concept, with a learning readiness unit for children two to four years old, and another for older children. There are also supplemental materials. www.fiveinarow.com.

List 2.9. The Principle Approach – Christian

The last method we discuss is for Christians who wish to follow seven Biblical principles in raising and teaching their children.

"There is a revival bubbling up in America—a healing in our land. It is a revival of America's Christian history and a desire to learn those Biblical principles, which identify America as a Christian nation with a Christian form of government." This quote is taken from the book *Teaching and Learning America's Christian History: The Principle Approach*, by Rosalie Slater (Foundation for American Christian Education, 1984). Those who adhere to this approach believe the United States was founded on Christian principles and wish to bring back Christian leadership to the government and country.

The principle approach (PA) is based on the following seven Biblical principles:

1. God-given individuality
2. Christian self-government
3. Character (Biblical New Testament)
4. Conscience
5. A Christian form of government
6. Local self-government
7. A restoration of (Christian) unity in government

Proponents of this approach, which is highly political, believe that Christian leadership must be restored to the United States and the world. The academics are taught from a biblical point of view with the quality of a classical education.

Here are some of the best resources for the principle approach:

- *The Forerunner.* This website contains the complete article by Rosalie Slater quoted earlier. It also includes the list of seven principles, with explanations for each. www.forerunner.com.
- *Principle Approach.org.* There is a great deal of information on this website about starting a principle approach homeschool and a PA conference, as well as already existing conferences and other resources. It also discusses the non-teaching of America's Christian history in public schools for many years. www.principleapproach.org.
- *Foundation for American Christian Education.* FACE is connected to www.principle approach.org. This contains the heart of the PA and its resources. It includes information on making a private school based on the PA. www.face.net.

Part Three

Subjects and Lesson Plans

List 3.1. Language Arts and English

This section includes the following subject areas:

A. Reading and Phonics Resources
B. Spelling Resources
C. Vocabulary Resources – Word Roots
D. Grammar Resources
E. Penmanship Resources
F. Writing – Composition Resources

List 3.1A. Reading and Phonics Resources

Phonics—the study of the sounds of letters as they are used in words—is the first language art your child will encounter. Since the early 1940s, some researchers have tried to develop alternatives to learning to read by phonics—*whole language* or *whole word* being the label placed on phonics-alternative systems. Some students have learned to read using whole word systems, but the overwhelming majority of people who are "good" readers and spellers have a basis in phonics. (It also makes it easier to learn a foreign language.) Some of the programs listed here are pure phonics programs; others teach phonics and then go on to other language arts applications as well. All of these programs are suitable for pre-kindergarten to grade five or higher, unless otherwise specified.

- *ABC Read.* A package of three different elements that will help children or adults learn to read. Flash cards, three hours of recorded lessons on DVD or VHS, and a printed list of over 1,650 words that are also included on an audio cassette tape. www.homeschoolreading.com.
- *America's Phonics.* This program combines traditional instruction with computer instruction to achieve the goal of literacy. The student begins with the basics, phonics, and then progresses through worksheets and, ultimately, computer exercises, through an exposure to parts of speech, comprehension, and reading. 106 Stonehaven Rd., McKinney, TX 75070; 214-592-9798; amphonics@sbcglobal.net; www.americasphonics.com.
- *Phonics Tutor.* This highly praised program, developed by Dr. David Hickerson, offers an excellent foundation in phonics awareness. The first part of the program can by used by a four-year-old with adult supervision and by a six-year-old without it. Phonics Tutor includes both books and CD-ROMs and provides children with an approach that lets them begin reading words, phrases, and sentences virtually right away, providing interest and enthusiasm. Phonics Tutor is also highly recommended for use with those students with dyslexia or other reading disabilities. 4:20 Communications, Inc., P.O. Box 421027, Minneapolis, MN 55442-0027; 888-420-7323; www.phonics tutor.com.
- *Centrifuge Language Arts Curriculum.* Centrifuge has created a complete K–12 program for teaching all of the language arts, from phonics, spelling, and elementary reading through poetry, writing upper grade English, and penmanship. 3611 C.R. 100, Hesperus, CO 81326; 800-900-1907; www.centricurriculum.com.
- *Phonics Pathways* (grades K–2). This is one of the most respected and highly regarded phonics learning systems in homeschooling. The

upcoming ninth edition of Phonics Pathways will retain the same content as the previous edition, but will feature many new additions, including many reproducible games, a step-by-step spelling guide, teacher/student record sheets, and new details showing how Phonics Pathways aligns with most state standards. It is perfect for teaching your young child the basics of reading and spelling. 800-956-7739; www.josseybass.com.

- *Paradigm Publishing.* Since 1984, this company has produced one of the best and most-applauded phonics-teaching programs of all time, Dr. Sam Blumenfeld's Alpha-Phonics. They also publish other language arts products by Dr. Blumenfeld, including his book *How to Tutor.* phonics@howtotutor.com; www.alphaphonics.com and also www.howtotutor.com.

- *Sing, Spell, Read & Write.* This very popular and well-known computer-based program utilizes phonics as its base and then takes the user to complete reading mastery in thirty-six steps. For more information, the website provides contact information on a state-by-state basis. At www.pearsonlearning.com, click "Phonics."

- *Go Phonics.* This is a complete language arts curriculum for K–12. It includes forty-eight phonics games, six volumes of stories, key word charts, a songbook with audio CD, and much other material. Foundations for Learning, LLC; 800-553-5950 or 509-687-1513; www.gophonics.com.

- *Click N Read.* An online program that offers three reasonable monthly installments for a lifetime subscription. For parents who do not mind computer-based learning, this is very attractive and affordable, too. 5737 Kanan Road, Ste. 107, Agoura Hills, CA 91301; 877-254-2522; www.clicknkids.com.

- *Lost Classics Books* (Emma Serl series). LCB reprints classic books that have gone out of print—some for many years. They offer an excellent line, by Emma Serl, that covers all early language arts skills, right up to middle school age: phonics, reading, grammar, spelling, punctuation—everything, in attractive and sturdy, hardcover, old-fashioned books first published in the 1800s. Lost Classics also offers a wide variety of other "lost" books, including an excellent series on American history for grades 4–7. 888-611-2665; www.lostclassicsbooks.com.

- *Flipping for Phonics* (grades K–4). This unique approach to teaching phonics is a cascading, spiral-bound book, with six tiers for each letter sound, enabling the combinations for two thousand words in all and allowing the child to stay focused on sounding out the next letter, rather than searching for the information. This is perfect for kinetic learners, with colorful pictures representing the sounds. www.flippingforphonics.com.

- *Phonics Road to Reading and Spelling* (grades K–5). This is a complete phonics program that also places strong emphasis on the abilities of spelling and speaking, as well as reading. Phonics Road is designed to aid the child to learn to think and make intellectual connections that will be useful in later academics—especially Latin and English. The parent training text is on video. Schola Publications, 1698 Market St. #162, Redding, CA 96001; ph. 530-275-2064; fax 530-275-9151; www.thephonicsroad.com.

List 3.1B. Spelling Resources

Spelling comes naturally to some students but only with great effort to others. Some people have learning disabilities in actually processing what they see, such as dyslexia, and often a difficulty with spelling is the first indication of such a condition. Each spelling program available has different strengths, depending on the type of learner your child is and what his or her problems—if any—may be.

Often, a thorough grounding in the study of phonics will help the student master spelling very easily. This is one of the reasons that many homeschooling families use a phonics approach—it is an excellent foundation for all language skills to come.

Contrary to popular belief, computer program spell-checkers are not foolproof. A word can be spelled correctly but still not be the word you intended to use, or the checker may simply fail to find an error that a human speller would see. It is always risky to rely 100 percent on spell-checkers. Here are some excellent spelling products for all types of learners, including dyslexic and hearing-impaired students.

- *Making Spelling Sense* and *Making Spelling Sense II* (grades 3–6). These two volumes, by a highly respected educational author, Bonnie Terry, enable the student user to develop the ability to spell over five hundred of the most-used words in English, using eight basic spelling patterns and highlighting the few words that do not fit into the eight patterns, so that they can be learned by sight. Ms. Terry's goal is to make spelling make sense by a step-by-step sequential approach. Bonnie Terry Learning, 238 Poet Smith Dr., Auburn, CA 95603; 530-888-7160; www.bonnieterrylearning.com.

- *Fifteen Minutes a Day for Spelling Power* (grades 3–6). This excellent book, originally published in 1994, will show your student how to spell the five thousand most-used words in only fifteen minutes per day, divided into three segments of five minutes each. The first segment is spent reviewing the Word Flow Lists; the second segment, studying misspelled words from the Word List; the last segment is spent performing skill-building drills and activities that will reinforce spelling knowledge. Castlemoyle Books, P.O. Box 520, Pomeroy, WA 99347; orders, 888-SPELL-86; 509-843-5009; www.castlemoyle.com.

- *The Spelling Doctor* (Raymond Laurita) (grades 1–12+). This website features many interesting products to teach reading and improve spelling. Mr. Laurita has been researching and writing works about English and learning its various skills for over forty years and offers much useful and interesting information beyond reading or spelling, covering the entire spectrum of English. P.O. Box 1326, Camden, ME 04843; 207-236-8649; www.spellingdoctor.com.

- *How to Teach Spelling* (grades 1–12). This site contains many interesting products, including spelling tiles, accompanying textbooks, phonogram cards (containing consonant or vowel blends) and an interactive CD-ROM. If you are actively searching for spelling materials, this site deserves a close inspection. There is even a free demo of the CD. www.all-about-spelling.com.

- *AVKO Spelling & Dyslexia Foundation* (grades 1 to adult). Don McCabe is one of the foremost authorities on developing products to aid those with dyslexia and other learning disabilities in all areas of reading and spelling skills. The AVKO website offers many excellent materials for homeschoolers, including a spelling program (with samples available at the site), a reading program, and a penmanship program. AVKO Educational Research Foundation, 3084 W. Willard Road, Suite W, Clio, MI 48420-7801; 866-AVKO-612; www.spelling.org.

- *The Phonetic Zoo* (grades 1–8). Andrew Pudewa is a homeschooling father of six and also a master at teaching—he understands the difficulties young minds have in grasping and then mastering various concepts of English. His phonics-based spelling program, The Phonetic Zoo, is a perfect way for homeschooling parents to teach their children to spell. It includes a twenty-eight-minute video for the parents to watch first, demonstrating what they will be required to do. There are rule cards and CD-ROM lessons for the child to listen to and a self-checking section of each lesson to aid your child in seeing what, if anything, was wrong. Institute for Excellence in Writing, P.O. Box 6065, Atascadero, CA 93423; 800-856-5815; info@writing-edu.com; www.writing-edu.com.

- *Wizardsspell* (grades 1–8). This is a unique product to encourage the practice of spelling skills in students. It is not a curriculum or how-to-teach method for learning to spell, but rather an online, multisensory, interactive spelling program that encourages practice. Wizardsspell was developed by a mother whose daughter was not learning how to spell because of problems in auditory processing, so she developed a program that was visual and active. Her daughter's spelling improved and so has that of many other children who have used the program. It provides self-checking and automatic tracking of results and improvement. For parents, it removes much of the worry and stress out of teaching spelling—especially to children with any sort of learning disability or problem with spelling. The child can practice independently with Wizardsspell and is likely to find its multisensory environment enjoyable. 244 Shannonbrook Lane, Frederick, MD 21702; 703-742-8404; www.wizardsspell.com.

List 3.1C. Vocabulary Resources – Word Roots

Learning the Latin and Greek roots for our English words is an essential and excellent beginning vocabulary study. The extensive number of words in our language that are based on these two ancient languages makes a study of their word roots as foundational to vocabulary as a study of phonics is to spelling and reading. Many SAT prep instructors also note that students with a knowledge of Latin and Greek word roots demonstrate a higher proficiency in the language skills areas and therefore tend to achieve higher scores on the exam. The following products offer a wide variety of learning options:

- *English from the Roots Up, Vols. I and II* (Literacy Unlimited) (grades 4–10). The motto of the publisher is "When you know a little Latin and Greek, you know a lot of English"—and their books set out to enable your child to do just that. The books are easy to use and an enjoyable way to discover many of our language's roots and expand the vocabulary greatly. A video and a game are also available from the company. Literacy Unlimited; www.literacyunlimited.com.
- *Word Roots* (Critical Thinking) (grades 4–10). Program includes CD-ROMs and accompanying books. This program offers Latin and Greek word roots and prefixes and suffixes. For parents who are not averse to computer-based learning, this product is excellent and effective. It allows the flexibility of software programs, in that reviews and tests are easy and the graphics are often pleasing and interesting. Critical Thinking Company, P.O. Box 1610, Seaside, CA 93955-1610; 800-458-4849; www.criticalthinking.com.
- *Latin & Greek Word Roots, Vols. 1 and 2* (grades 6–12). Designed for middle and high school students who need help in the language arts. Glavach & Associates, P.O. Box 547, Healdsburg, CA 95448; 707-894-5047; www.strugglingreaders.com.
- *Hey, Andrew, Teach Me Some Greek* (Greek N Stuff). This complete Koine Greek program teaches the student biblical Greek to use in translating the New Testament. Although it is really overkill for a word-root study, it will provide the student with an abundance of such information. The company also has a Latin program. Greek N Stuff; 309-796-2707; www.greeknstuff.com.
- *The Spelling Doctor* (Raymond Laurita) (grades 5–12). Mr. Laurita's website contains many interesting products to teach reading and improve spelling. Mr. Laurita has been researching and writing works about English and learning its various skills for over forty years and offers much useful and interesting information beyond reading or spelling, but covering the entire spectrum of English. This site offers extensive information on Latin and Greek word roots and how to spell them in English, when they have become different. P.O. Box 1326, Camden, ME 04843; 207-236-8649; www.spellingdoctor.com.

List 3.1D. Grammar Resources

Of all the language arts, grammar is the most mysterious to most of us. Grammar is the study of the basic building blocks of our language—words—in actual use, rather than just as part of a word list for spelling or as the end result of a group of sounds. Phonics teaches a person how to identify the sounds we use to make up our language, both spoken and written; once a word is placed in a context—in a sentence—it then has a function, known as a part of speech. This is what grammar deals with: words in use, in action.

These products will aid the teaching parent greatly in removing the mystery of grammar—at least to teach your child! Because our language is constantly growing and adding new words—or new uses, mainly—grammar will never cease to have a mysterious, growing quality, too. But at least you can teach the foundations to your child without stress and actually enjoy yourself as well!

- *Jensen's Grammar* (grades 5–12). This book, written by Frode Jensen, master wordsmithy, states that "grammar is a means, not an end." With that in mind, the student can dive right in to a serious study of the basic element of all writing: the sentence. Mr. Jensen writes with wit and real-life knowledge—he recalls what it was like to be a student—and he communicates his knowledge in an attractive and easy way. But he stresses that the book is not easy. It is hard work. He offers lessons that repeat and review what has been learned before, and new ideas and concepts are added in increments to make them palatable. Contact information for this and the following two books: 1355 Ferry Road, Grant's Pass, OR 97526; 541-476-3080 or 541-474-9756; www.jsgrammar.com.
- *Journey Through Grammar Land* (grades 5–9). By Frode Jensen, suited for fifth-grade students and up or those who have not fared well with other grammar approaches.
- *Jensen's Punctuation* (grades 7 to adult). Also by Frode Jensen. Mr. Jensen admits to referring to his own book when faced with a tricky bit of punctuation!
- *The Sentence Zone Card Game* (grades 3–8). If you are looking for an entertaining way to boost your child's knowledge of sentence structure, Bonnie Terry, M.Ed., has written a great learning game for you! The Sentence Zone contains six levels of play for learners from the youngest to advanced scholars of grammar. The game consists of fourteen different colored cards, each containing a part of a sentence—noun, verb, and so on. The object of the game is to look through the cards that are available and construct a sentence. As the other parts of speech are introduced, the sentences become more

difficult to create. The Sentence Zone will be useful for many years, as it begins with very young grammar students and proceeds all the way up to sixth or seventh grade—and even beyond, providing an occasional review. Bonnie Terry Learning, 38 Poet Smith Dr., Auburn, CA 95603; ph.: 530-888-7160; www.bonnieterrylearning.com.

- *Applications of Grammar* (grades 7–12). This series of six reasonably priced workbooks, answer keys, and test packets by Christian Liberty Press (CLP), one of the foremost Christian publishers in the country, offers an excellent and thorough grammar course to the Christian homeschooling family. Workbooks run from 155 to 336 pages, depending on the grade level. The CLP course ranges from providing instruction and exercises in grammar concepts and uses for middle school–aged students up to advanced composition work for the student on the threshold of college writing. Christian Liberty Press, 502 W. Euclid Ave, Arlington Heights, IL 60004; 800-832-2741; http://ebiz.netopia.com/clpress. Catalog request: www.christianlibertypress.com.
- *Bob Jones English and Grammar Course* (grades 2–12). One of the powerhouses in Christian curriculum publishing for many, many years, BJU Press provides an excellent line of English and grammar kits for use from the very beginning student up to high school seniors. BJ University Press; www.bjupress.com.

List 3.1E. Penmanship Resources

In this age of computer-based work, it is important to remember that handwriting is still a basic, necessary skill. Many times a computer is not available to a person who must write notes for later use or write a complete draft of a document for later computer rendering, or who may simply wish to provide a personal touch by handwriting a letter to someone! The SAT and similar assessment exams require the test-taker to handwrite essay answers. A legible, fast handwriting ability is still essential, and these products help the homeschooled child develop this skill.

- *Barchowsky Fluent Handwriting* (grades 1–7). Nan Jay Barchowsky developed her method imparting fluidity and speed, based on more than twenty years' experience teaching handwriting—seventeen of them in classrooms—and her materials and method of teaching have won praise from homeschoolers all over the country. P.O. Box 117, Aberdeen, MD 21001; ph. 410-272-0836; twenty-four-hour fax ordering, 410-297-9767; www.bfhhandwriting.com.
- *Peterson Directed Handwriting* (grades 1–7). Rand Nelson has many years' experience working to develop new and unique handwriting tools that increase fluidity and ease of penmanship. In addition to his actual method of handwriting, he offers interesting tools such as pencil grips to protect young hands and fine motor muscles from pain and discomfort and from forming bad habits when holding pencils. See his online store for the complete line of books and accessories. 315 S. Maple Ave., Greensburg, PA 15601; 724-837-4900; www.peterson-handwriting.com/reply.html.
- *Startwrite Software* (grades 1–4). This company has created an interesting bridge between the "old" skill of handwriting and the "new" technology of the computer. The software program creates the dotted letters that beginning students of handwriting use to trace over. The user can choose from a wide variety of fonts and writing styles, print a sheet or two or three of dotted letters in that font and style, and voila! the student has hours of practice material to work with. This program saves hours of shopping in educational stores for a book filled with dotted letters in one font, one style. www.startwrite.com.
- *Handwriting Without Tears* (grades pre-K–5). HWT offers award-winning programs to teach the art of handwriting—both printing and cursive—to young writers. Readiness, with practice of shapes and fine motor skills, is begun in the first section, pre-K. Printing is covered in grades 1–2 and cursive in grades 3–4, with a review in grade 5, which can also be used as a remedial program for older students who need to practice and perfect

their cursive writing. Jan Olsen, OTR 8001 MacArthur Blvd, Cabin John, MD 20818; 301-263-2700; www.hwtears.com.

- *Portland State University – Continuing Education Press* (grades K–6). Getty-Dubay Italic Handwriting Series, grades K–6 and adult. This handwriting system was developed to be loop-free, making it legible and fast. The creators also offer free handwriting seminars. Check the PSU CEP website for information about the program and free seminars given by the creators. Getty-Dubay; www.cep.pdx.edu.

List 3.1F. Writing – Composition Resources

English composition is another subject that can seem daunting to homeschooling parents. Many adults recall the terror they experienced in the middle grades when the teacher would announce "Today, we are going to write a paper" or when faced with a book report that was looming and they were stuck, staring at a blank page for hours, not knowing where to begin.

Today's homeschooling parents have excellent writing programs to aid them, so the terror they recall can be a thing of the past. Some very gifted and enlightened teachers have developed complete writing curriculums, allowing the parent and children to work together and then have the children work on their own.

- *Institute for Excellence in Writing* (IEW) (CD-ROMs) (grades 5–12). The IEW writing program, created by masterful teacher Andrew Pudewa, is a series of lessons with CD-ROM lectures by Andrew and textbook lessons with assignments and explanations that coincide with the lectures. This creates an enjoyable atmosphere for learning the fine art of composition. Mr. Pudewa is a much-sought-after conference speaker, and his ability to communicate verbally is one of the keys to the excellence of this program. He speaks well and clearly, with a mastery of his subject that commands one's attention immediately. The IEW website also offers other excellent products developed by Andrew Pudewa, including Teaching the Classics and Poetry Memorization. IEW, P.O. Box 6065, Atascadero, CA 93423; 800-856-5815; www.writing-edu.com.
- *Ten Minutes to Better Study Skills* and *The Writer's Easy Reference Guide* (grades 6–12). These books by Bonnie Terry aim to improve writing and study skills at the same time. *Ten Minutes* teaches effective note-taking, organized thinking, conversion of notes to articles, and improvement of one's writing techniques. *Easy Reference* provides quick-to-find information on types of sentences, steps in the writing process, and much more that will take the anxiety out of mastering the craft of writing. Bonnie Terry has thirty years' experience teaching, and all of her products are enjoyable and very effective. 238 Poet Smith Dr., Auburn, CA 95603; 530-888-7160; www.bonnieterrylearning.com.
- *Writing Strands* (grades 5–12). This writing composition series of eleven books was developed by homeschooling dad and college professor David Marks when he and his wife were homeschooling their own son, who is now a college professor himself. The Writing Strands books have been used for many years and have produced excellent results for homeschooling families all over the world. In addition to the popular writing composition series, Writing Strands also offers a seven-volume Reading series and a speech book, teaching effective

verbal and nonverbal communication in an informal setting. National Writing Institute, 624 W. University #248, Denton, TX 76201-1889; 800-688-5375; www.writing-strands.com.

- *Writing to Change the World: How to Style Your Writing for Publication*, by Susan Brown. This unique volume shows the older student writer, approximately ninth through twelfth grades, how to write with an eye toward being published, not simply to satisfy a lesson plan or teacher assignment that goes into a desk drawer or the trash can. Available from Jensen's Wordsmiths; 1355 Ferry Road, Grant's Pass, OR 97526; 541-476-3080 or 541-474-9756; www.jsgrammar.com.

- *Write Shop* (grades 6–10). Write Shop is one of the most popular incremental writing programs among homeschoolers of junior and senior high school ages. It teaches the basics of all types of writing, including narrative, persuasive, descriptive, and essay. 5753 Klusman Ave, Alta Loma, CA 91737; 909-989-5576; www.writeshop.com.

- *Five Finger Paragraph* (grades K–12). Is writing an essay intimidating to your child or yourself? Ms. Johnnie Lewis has a solution for you in her series of books on mastering the essay form. The SAT, ACT, and CEB all require applicants to write essays on the spot, so developing confidence and skill for this area alone is important. 1860 Sandy Plains Road, Murrietta, GA 30066; 770-977-4185; www. thefivefingerparagraph.com.

- *Final Draft* (Screenwriting Software & Teacher Workbook) (grades 6 and up). Although this company's products are known to screenwriters the world over, its use as a creative writing tool is virtually unknown and unthought-of. However, as anyone who has ever written a script knows, the form—for plays and the screen—is an excellent one for learning the craft of writing. The new Teacher Workbook coincides with materials already contained on the Final Draft software program and takes the student through the processes of character development, plot building, outlining, visualizing, and more, with exercises for building each skill. Final Draft, Inc., 26707 W. Agoura Rd., Suite 205, Calabasas, CA 91302; www.finaldraft.com.

List 3.2. Geography Resources

Geography has been cited repeatedly as one of the great weaknesses of American school children. The oft-told stories of public high school students not being able to locate such areas as Japan or even Britain or Europe have shocked many homeschool parents and made them determined that their children will know geography. Here are some excellent resources to accomplish that end:

- *Mapping the World by Heart* (grades 5–12). Mapping the World by Heart has been around for many years and has proven to be a popular package for learning geography. It presents world geography in small pieces that can be easily assimilated. Students learn to draw and label the physical location of countries, land, and water. The kit comprises maps of nine regions and blank maps of the regions—enough to last an entire school year, plus teacher's guide and introductory video. Tom Snyder Productions, 100 Talcott Ave, Watertown, MA 02472-5703; 800-342-0236; www.tomsnyder.com.
- *Geography Matters* (grades 5–12). This website caters to the sensibilities of homeschoolers. It offers a number of unique geography curricula, including Bible geography, U.S. geography, and world geography. There are also atlases, many enticing geography games, and history materials. You can teach historical geography with these products—a fascinating way to cover two subjects that will light up your child's imagination. Geography Matters, P.O. Box 92, Nancy, KY 42544; 606-636-4678; www.geomatters.com.
- *Runkle Geography* (grades 6–12). This company is responsible for *Welcome to the Wonderful World of Geography*, a three-part series for sixth through twelfth grades, consisting of the textbook, the student workbook, and the teacher's guide. The Runkle series now carried by Geography Matters is the original, written by Barbara Runkle, who has produced quality geography products in the homeschool world for many years. Geography Matters, P.O. Box 92, Nancy, KY 42544; 606-636-4678; www.runklepub.com.
- *The Science Chef: Travels Around the World* (ages 8–12). If you are studying world geography and would like to supplement your textbook with a novel way, try this book by Joan D'Amico. She provides more than sixty easy-to-prepare recipes and food experiments. Ms. D'Amico also provides a nutrition guide, and she keeps kitchen safety utmost throughout her book. For beginners to advanced cooks. Available from Amazon.com or Overstock.com.

List 3.3. History Resources

For parents who enjoy creating their own lesson plans and finding materials, many of these resources are excellent. They provide research and other pertinent historical information that allow the parent to either teach from the computer, develop materials from ideas on the Internet, or obtain books from the library.

- *Bright Ideas Press* (grades 5–12) (Christian). This company, owned by a homeschooling family, publishes many fascinating Bible-based history volumes, relating to both world history and U.S. history. The family's oldest son, J. B., is serving in the U.S. infantry in Iraq and has written a book *From Basic to Baghdad: A Soldier Writes Home.* Bright Ideas Press, P.O. Box 333, Cheswold, DE 19936; 877-492-8081; www.brightideaspress.com.
- *Peace Hill Press* (grades 4–8). Professor Susan Wise Bauer is one of the most skilled writers of history in the homeschooling genre. In addition to having been homeschooled herself, she is a homeschooling mom and a professor at William & Mary College. Her four-volume series *The Story of the World* is an excellent way to gain a fast, clear insight into the unfolding of world history from ancient times to 1994. Much of history does not require the ponderous detail that so many books devote to it. Peace Hill Press also offers test booklets for *The Story of the World* and other books by Susan Wise Bauer, including *The Well-Trained Mind.* Peace Hill Press, 18021 The Glebe Lane, Charles City, VA 23030; 877-322-3445 or 804-829-5043; www.peacehillpress.net.
- *Greenleaf Press* (grades 4–12) (Christian). Greenleaf is a highly respected purveyor of homeschooling books and materials. Owners Rob and Cindy Shear are Christian homeschooling parents of a large family in the Nashville, Tennessee, area. They provide excellent resources in all phases of history, ancient to modern. See their extensive catalog at their website. 3761 Hwy 109 North, Lebanon, TN 37087; 615-449-1617; www.greenleafpress.com.
- *Bluestocking Press* (grades 5–12). For more than ten years this company has published the famous "Uncle Eric" series of books, which teach history about multiple topics. For instance, in *Whatever Happened to Penny Candy?* Richard Maybury ("Uncle Eric") uses historical events from ancient Rome to explain modern economic principles. Another is *Evaluating Books: What Would Thomas Jefferson Think About This?* in which Mr. Maybury offers insights into principles of economics, government, and history. He also writes about World War I and II and the Thousand Year War in the Middle East. Bluestocking offers many other excellent books by other authors as well. P.O. Box

1014, Placerville, CA 95667-1014; 800-959-8586 or 530-622-8586; www.bluestockingpress.com.

- *Drive Thru History* (Video/DVD) (grades 5–10) (Christian). This well-known video series, presented by National Day of Prayer, is now in its fifth installment—*Drive Thru History, America.* Hosted by David Stotts, it takes the viewer from one historical spot to another, with intelligent, humorous narration, explaining the events and people that were of significance at the location and how it affected our world. The other four volumes of the series cover Rome, Greece, and Turkey, for an insight into the ancient world. Write c/o National Day of Prayer Task Force, P.O. Box 15616, Colorado Springs, CO 80935-5616; ph. 719-531-3379; fax 719-548-452; www.dthamerica.com.

- *The Lukeion Project* (online Greece and Rome class) (grades 9–12). This unique history resource offers students the opportunity to study ancient Greece and Rome in a real-time, online classroom with two real live "dirt" archeologists, Regan and Amy Barr. The Barrs spent ten years in the Mediterranean region, digging, snapping photos, and studying the lives and times of ancient peoples in this area. This is not an online tutorial, but an actual interactive "class"; students can communicate with the Barrs during class or privately. Students also have access to a class web page with review, games, quizzes, and other activities. www.lukeion.org.

- *Vision Forum* (grades 3–8) (Christian). This historical website focuses on American history, from the Pilgrims to Roy Rogers. There is the All-American Boys' Adventure Catalog, featuring costumes and accessories such as a real coonskin cap, and the Beautiful Girlhood Collection of virtuous girlhood costumes, dresses, accessories, diverse products, and books. Vision Forum believes in the pre-1900s concept of righteous womanhood and manhood and aims to help parents who wish to promote these traditional values. www.visionforum.com.

- *Learning Through History Magazine* (age 9 to adult). Every other month, a sixty-four-page issue of *LTH* is available to subscribers, overflowing with unique articles, arts and crafts projects ideas, hands-on activities, study guides for historical literature, discussion questions, web links, and suggested books and videos all relating to one historical theme per issue. Every issue of *Learning Through History* has something for every history student, whether voracious or reluctant. Subscribers also receive bonuses in the form of e-books relevant to a historical period. Classic Education, Inc., P.O. Box 110129, Naples, FL 34108; 239-261-5100; www.learningthroughhistory.com.

- *Adventure Tales of America: An Illustrated History of America* (grades 5–8); Vol. 1, 1492–1877, 364 pp., hardcover; Vol. 2, 1876–1932, 394 pp., hardcover. This set is highly acclaimed by users, especially those students who have ADHD or similar attention issues. The pages are arranged so as to be easily read and assimilated. The publisher also offers many supplemental products to Vol. 1, such as a teacher's guide, student activities book, CD-ROM Constitution game, three audio cassettes— Revolution, Constitutional Convention, and Abraham Lincoln—and six wall posters depicting various aspects of American history covered in the book. Vol. 2 offers a teacher's guide supplement. Signal Media Publishers; adventuretales@signalmedia.com; www.adventuretales.com.

List 3.4. Math Resources

Along with the middle-level and higher sciences, math is the "scariest" topic a homeschooling parent can confront. History, geography, even English can be faced with courage, but math is often the weakest subject parents remember from their own school experience. Being faced with teaching one's child the same mysterious subject is almost too much!

Fortunately, the modern-day homeschooling world is filled with great resources for teaching math. Many dedicated math teachers have put forth the time and energy to create all sorts of math-teaching materials. In addition to the traditional books, there are CD-ROM or video programs and even a card game for learning math. Parents, fear no more and read on!

- *Homeschoolmath.net* (grades 1–5). Homeschool Math is a resource site for learning elementary math. Parents can create free worksheets and find teaching tips, free lesson plans, and links to games, quizzes, and interactive tutorials. www.homeschoolmath.net.
- *Creative Teaching Associates.* A great family homeschooling site to find math and science games. Creative Teaching Associates offers plenty of activities based on problem solving, algebra, languages, fractions, literature, and more. www.mastercta.com.
- *Singapore Math.com, Inc.* (grades 2–6). Since 1998, SingaporeMath. com has been committed to bringing quality educational books to U.S. schools and homeschoolers. The main offering of the company is the Primary Mathematics U.S. Edition Series, emphasizing concept development, mental techniques, and problem solving. The time-tested program presents interesting concepts and clearly written explanations. 404 Beavercreek Road, #225, Oregon City, OR 97045; 503-557-8100; www.singaporemath.com.
- *Easy Math Reference Guide* (grades 5–12). Developed by Bonnie Terry, M.Ed., an educator with over thirty years' experience teaching regular education and special education students, the BT *Easy Math Reference Guide* presents math in a logical progression, clearly explaining basic math calculations and progressing to more advanced topics. Once students build a basic math foundation, they learn to calculate area, perimeter, and ratio and learn to recognize and perform calculations involving various geometric shapes, lines, and angles. Along the way, the guide provides useful tips and tricks to help students perform accurate calculations. Published by Bonnie Terry Learning, 238 Poet Smith Dr., Auburn, CA 95603; 530-888-7160; www.bonnieterrylearning.com.
- *www.mastercta.com.* A great family homeschooling site to find math and science games. Creative Teaching Associates offers plenty of activities

based on problem solving, algebra, languages, fractions, literature, and more.

- *Learning Upgrade* (grades 6–12). Learning Upgrade offers reasonably priced, award-winning learning programs to teach reading, writing, and math by using songs, videos, and games. The three revolutionary online courses currently offered are Math Upgrade, Reading Upgrade, and Comprehension Upgrade. Math Upgrade covers basic math through pre-algebra and early geometry. The program was developed by a creative team of teachers, musicians, artists, and programmers, dedicated to motivating students to complete the lessons. 2034 Ridge Crest Place, Escondido, CA 92029; 800-998-8864; www.learningupgrade.com.

- *Teaching Tape Technology* (grades 3–12) (Saxon Math on video/DVD). Teaching Tape Technology offers a series of two-hour VHS and DVD presentations designed to complement Saxon Math books. Following the format of Saxon Math books, visually appealing and easy-to-follow instruction is presented in a self-paced, no-pressure video format. Certified instructors clearly explain and demonstrate each math concept. In addition, each video is full of helpful hints and shortcuts to reduce student work time but not student comprehension. 9975 Chemstrand Rd., Pensacola, FL 32514; 850-475-7860; www.teachingtape.com.

- *Math Drawings* (grades 4 and older). This unique and engaging program offers a multidisciplinary method of teaching math principles through the use of art. Math Drawings includes a series of clearly written, step-by-step instructions that allow students to create up to four drawings using only basic geometric shapes. Students who can draw a straight line with a ruler will be amazed at how easily they can produce a detailed drawing using the principles of Math Drawings. This proven method of teaching solidifies math concepts and opens the door to student creativity. P.O. Box 801, Woodland Hills, CA 91365; 818-887-5611; www.mathdrawings.com.

- *The Math Zone* (grades 3–8). This math card game is an exciting and fun way for any age group to learn and practice basic math skills. Once again, Bonnie Terry has succeeded in taking students beyond the routine completion of pages and pages of math problems and into the world of educational games. Armed with three color-coded decks of cards, students use adding, multiplying, subtracting, and dividing to learn how numbers shrink and grow. The game is designed to allow multiple players of varying skill levels to play simultaneously with an equal opportunity to win. Every flip of a card offers a new learning opportunity, and no player can claim victory until the final card is played and the final calculation is made. Published by Bonnie Terry Learning, 238 Poet Smith Dr., Auburn, CA 95603; 530-888-7160; www.bonnieterrylearning.com.

- *Systematic Mathematics* (grades 6–9). Developed by educator Paul Ziegler, Systematic Math is an affordable program that helps children understand math, not merely memorize numbers. It is provided in DVD format and can be used by all members of the household without the need to purchase any additional materials. Instruction modules consist of fifteen to forty-five lessons that systematically develop a particular math concept. Each carefully developed module is designed to motivate students and help them realize that math has real-world applications. Also available is Rescue Math, a fifty-two-lesson course designed to provide older students with a math foundation allowing them to continue on to algebra and beyond. East 13902 County Road ZZ, Ontario, WI 54651; 866-532-7648; www.systemath.com.
- *Professor B's Power Math* (grades K–7). This unique program activates children's universal gift for learning math and enables them to master the subject. Commonsense components and carefully verbalized explanations are used to help students of all ages raise their math proficiency. Presented in CD format, Power Math enables almost anyone to learn and teach math simultaneously. P.O. Box 2079, Duluth, GA 30096; 800-847-6284; www.profb.com.
- *The Art of Problem Solving* (grades 7 and up). This company publishes a series of books, by Richard Rusczyk, for the serious math student. Rather than simply dealing with numbers and lists of problems, these volumes provide the method of thinking necessary for success in math and math-related endeavors. www.artofproblemsolving.com.

List 3.5. Science Resources

This section includes the following subject areas:

A. Biology and biological research
B. Chemistry
C. Astronomy
D. Earth science, geology, physics
E. Scientific visual aids and equipment
F. Science curriculum

In the field of general science, it is virtually impossible to find companies that specialize in only one discipline. Most science companies offer materials, books, hardware, software, and accessories in virtually every scientific field of endeavor. We have attempted to individualize the offerings where possible, but please search the listed websites thoroughly.

List 3.5A. Biology and Biological Research Resources

Homeschoolers of the early twenty-first century benefit greatly from the wealth of great science programs available, from doctor kits to digital dissecting software; complete microscope sets for gazing at the microcosm to complete telescope sets for viewing the macrocosm. Here are some that we have found to be very valuable.

- *The Apprentice Doctor* (grades 2–5). Apprentice Corporation presents a fascinating homeschool-friendly product designed to enthrall your physical science student or would-be future physician. It is a complete kit called the Apprentice Doctor, which is affordable and provides a great introduction to the world of the science of medicine to any child. It contains the traditional medical tools, such as a stethoscope, tongue depressors, penlight, eye chart, face masks—and a CD-ROM with an interactive "hospital." The Apprentice Doctor is a fascinating experiential learning aid for any child, but of course it's particularly suited for students interested in medicine as a career, whether as a physician, nurse, or one of the myriad other professionals at work today in the medical field as therapists, trainers, assistants, and so on. The Apprentice Corporation, 1051 Clinton Street, Buffalo, NY 14206; 716-853-3703; www.theapprenticedoctor.com.
- *Connecticut Valley Biological Supply Company* (grades 4–12). This family-owned business provides a wide variety of competitively priced science teaching materials for use in elementary through college level courses. Annelids, insects, crustaceans, and plants are just a few of the living organisms offered by Connecticut Valley. Extremely popular with their customers are Demoslides, a fast, easy way to study a variety of microlife. Demoslides are culture tubes filled with healthy living microorganisms. There is no need to open a Demoslide; a child can just put it under the microscope and start exploring. The cultures will last for several days, so Demoslides can be used over and over again. All of the cultures offered by Connecticut Valley are grown in the company laboratories under highly controlled conditions and are guaranteed to arrive in good condition. 800-628-7748; www.ctvalleybio.com.
- *Bio Corporation.* Bio Corporation specializes in providing affordable, high-quality preserved specimens, live specimens, dissection equipment, safety equipment, displays, books, manuals, educational movies and CDs, anatomical charts, and 3D models. Bio Corp offers a number of exotic specimens and provides for disposal of all specimens. 3911 Nevada St., Alexandria, MN 56308; 800-222-9094; www.biologyproducts.com.

- *Digital Frog International (DFI).* As you might guess from its quirky name, the flagship product of DFI is the award-winning Digital Frog 2. Basically, it's a virtual frog dissection program, but it's so much more than that. Besides being a worthy alternative to live dissection in a time of concern over widespread frog extinction, the software covers the ecology of eighteen different frog species, giving detailed notes about their lifecycle, behavior, and biodiversity. DFI also offers the next list item.

- *Digital Field Trips.* Enjoy an armchair exploratory trip to the Central American rain forests and the great deserts of North America with this CD-ROM. Trillium Place, RR#2, 7377 Calfass Rd., Puslinch, Ontario N0B 2J0, Canada; 519-766-1097; www.digitalfrog.com.

- *Mel Sobel Microscopes, Ltd.* (Microscope Store). Microscope Store offers the largest selection of new and used microscopes on the Internet. Unlike other online microscope dealers offering only one or two name brands, Microscope Store features microscopes, accessories, and digital and video systems from a variety of manufacturers, including Leica, Meiji Techno, Swift, Nikon, and Vanguard. The company also offers an exclusive line of Steindorff microscopes, as well as the complete line of Ohaus balances and an array of laboratory equipment. 29 Louis Street, Hicksville, NY 11801; 888-255-7267; www.microscopestore.com.

- *Professional Microscopes/MilesCo Scientific.* If you are in the market for a microscope or scope accessories of any type, and if you wish to see a vast array of microscopes and products to search through, see the website of MilesCo Scientific's Professional Microscopes, easily one of the largest suppliers of scopes and accessories in the country. 1006 3rd Street, International Falls, MN 56649; 218-285-3472 or 800-365-0838; www.professionalmicroscopes.com.

List 3.5B. Chemistry Resources

- *Quality Science Labs, LLC.* Quality Science Labs offers innovative laboratory curricula and corresponding chemistry and physical science kits to enhance the science learning experience, improve success, and aid teachers regardless of their teaching ability or science knowledge. These products are an excellent resource for homeschool parents who often find themselves teaching out of their field of expertise. From a teaching perspective, Quality Science Labs kits offer solid science. Kits are carefully designed and written by professors to intensify the non-laboratory curriculum component, simplify teaching, and empower the student to easily learn key scientific concepts. P.O. Box 162, Lake George, CO 80827; 866-700-1884; www.qualitysciencelabs.com.
- *Fascinating Science.* This company offers a system that consists of a series of thirty-two Internet-based, Flash-powered lessons on chemistry-related topics. Because the material exists in cyberspace, students have the opportunity to complete the lessons at their own pace, and in the comfort of their own home. 705 Kersey Road, Silver Spring, MD 20902; ph. 301-754-0888; fax 301-593-2183; www.fascinatingscience.com.

List 3.5C. Astronomy Resources

- *Starry Night Store.* Starry Night offers a vast array of stargazing equipment, including sky-viewing binoculars that allow you to see the Milky Way, Jupiter and its moons, even the Andromeda galaxy—inexpensively, without a telescope. They also offer a full line of telescopes, great astronomy software programs, and gadgets and accessories for anyone interested in this ever-growing realm of science. Starry Night, 89 Hangar Way, Watsonville, CA 95076; ph. 800-252-5417; fax 831-763-7024; www.starrynight.com.

- *Science Made Simple.* This website offers science information for many disciplines, not just astronomy. There are many excellent do-at-home science experiments and projects for science fairs. It provides basic science information for parents through a subscription-based online newsletter. It also serves as a central location for science products available through Amazon and other sites, which is very helpful if you don't know where else to look for novel things like a Star Theatre Home Planetarium or posters of the solar system. P.O. Box 503, Voorhees, NJ 08043; www.sciencemadesimple.com.

- *The Big Galaxy.* If you have a child who is obsessed by all things space, this is a great website for you! They offer books about space; a variety of space wall posters, including Space Rockets, several different solar system shots, and the night sky; space toys like Apollo astronauts and a mission control big box set; and inexpensive space school supplies, like a space pen, a space shuttle pencil sharpener, a solar system ruler, solar system pencil, and many more space-themed items. 800-966-5611 or 281-255-5522; www.thebiggalaxy.com.

- *Toy Soup.* Toy Soup offers yet another slant on astronomy-themed educational toys with great advanced items like a motorized solar system, a Home Theatre Planetarium, a solar system board game called Planet Quest, and a glow-in-the-dark solar system. Toy Soup also offers many other science toys and games, including Erector Sets and Smithsonian products. P.O. Box 1791, Clackamas, OR 97015; ph. 866-438-8080; fax 206-202-2545; www.toysoup.com.

- *Efston Science.* Located in Toronto, this is Canada's largest showroom of telescopes and novel astronomy equipment, with a vast array of scopes from every major manufacturer in the world, a complete robotics section, up-to-the-minute sky information on the website, and much more. On the website you can take a virtual tour of Efston's diverse departments, shop for anything you want related to star or sky gazing, and look at the current conditions as well. 3350 Dufferin Street, Toronto, Ontario M6A 3A4; 888-777-5255 or 416-787-4581; www.telescopes.ca.

List 3.5D. Earth Science, Geology, Physics Resources

- *ScienceLab.com.* This company offers some affordable and interesting products for the study of earth science—the National Geographic Earthquakes and Volcanoes Experiment Kit, for example. This is for ages ten and up and comes with a thirty-two-page booklet to guide the experiments. They also offer an interesting set of National Geographic Dinosaur Expedition products, the four Dinosaur Search kits. Each features a different type of dinosaur and includes a fossil dinosaur model in a plaster block, mallet and pick tool, chisel, brush, sponge, full-color instruction and fact sheet, dinosaur quiz fan, and three dinosaur fact cards. The student "unearths" the fossil using the same tools and techniques that real-life dinosaur hunters use. 14025 Smith Rd., Houston, TX 77396; 800-901-7247 or 281-441-4400; www.sciencelab.com.
- *Educational Activities, Inc.* EAI offers a number of interesting earth science DVDs and video products in the middle school age range. They cover topics from "Atoms" to "What Is Weather?" P.O. Box 87, Baldwin, NY 11510; 800-797-3223; www.edact.com.
- *Exploratorium.* One of the jewels of San Francisco, this state-of-the-art museum of science, art, and human perception offers a valuable website that is packed with science information and activities for anyone with Internet access. If you are ever near the Bay Area, visit the Exploratorium in person at 3601 Lyon Street, San Francisco, CA 94123; 415-EXP-LORE or for general information, 415-561-0360; www.exploratorium.edu.
- *National Park Service.* This website provides geology curriculum materials of various types, from online teacher guides and slideshows to activities and experiments you can do with your children. This is a great resource that our tax money makes possible. www2.nature.nps.gov/geology/education.
- *Science Kit & Boreal Laboratories.* SK carries a huge supply of scientific supplies and information for K–12 students and parent-teachers. Take some time to calmly search their website, as it contains a marvelous array of products. 777 E. Park Drive, P.O. Box 5003, Tonawanda, NY 14150; 800-828-7777; www.sciencekit.com.

List 3.5E. Scientific Visual Aids and Equipment

- *American 3B Scientific.* Most children are curious about the world around them, and are therefore, by nature, very interested in science. With proper tools and supplies, teachers and parents can encourage and stimulate this natural curiosity and interest. Based on the theory that "a model tells more than a thousand words," American 3B Scientific offers an impressive array of exciting products for educational training and teaching in the areas of medicine and health, physics, biology, and chemistry. 2189 Flintstone Dr., Unit O, Tucker, GA 30084; 770-492-9111; www.a3bs.com.

- *American Science & Surplus.* American Science & Surplus is a unique company that offers thousands of interesting regular—and some ever-changing—items, for very economical prices. They get in new shipments all the time, as befits any good surplus store, and their website and catalog should be reviewed often for new bargains. They have a great sense of humor, too, so reading their descriptions is entertaining in itself. 888-724-7587 or 847-647-0011; www.sciplus.com.

- *Arbor Scientific.* Arbor isn't owned or staffed by homeschoolers, but they design their products with classroom teachers in mind, based on the assumption that most teachers are not science teachers per se and therefore know little or nothing about presenting the subject. The same reasoning works for parents! www.arborsci.com.

- *Homeschoolingsupply.* A Canadian resource that contains virtually any product for any subject related to homeschooling. True Media Corp., 2350 Forbes St., Victoria, BC V8R 4B6; www.homeschoolingsupply.com.

- *Learning Things: The Education Store.* An amalgamation of discount-priced scientific gear for homeschoolers. Learning Things LLC, 1550 Oak Industrial Lane, Suite F, Cumming, GA 30041; 800-401-9931; www.homeschooldiscount.com.

- *Schoolmasters Science.* A great website for science kits and products. Schoolmasters Science has been providing science equipment and supplies to schools and individuals since 1954 and offers over two thousand items on its website. 745 State Circle, Ann Arbor, MI 48016; ph. 800-521-2832; fax 800-654-4321; www.schoolmasters.com/scicat.html.

- *WARD'S Homeschool, WARD'S Natural Science Establishment, LLC.* WARD'S has been providing the best in educational resources since 1862. The company was founded by Henry Augustus Ward, a world traveler who spanned the globe seven times in search of interesting phenomena, all in the name of scientific research. WARD'S carries on his legacy. 5100 West Henrietta Road, P.O. Box 92912, Rochester, NY 14692-9012; 800-962-2660; www.wardshomeschool.com/default.asp.

List 3.5F. Science Curriculum

- *Young Scientists Club.* YSC offers a sequential series of thirty-six science kits (with more to be added) by subscription—coming to your door once or twice a month. The series is suitable for ages four to twelve and is designed so that each kit builds on concepts that have been covered in the previous kit, offering new information and experiments and leading to the next kit. YSC removes the stress many parents feel in teaching science, providing you with the guidance and materials you need at a very affordable price. P.O. Box 634, Jamestown, RI 02835; 800-964-1320 or 401-423-2841; instructor@theyoungscientistclub.com; www.theyoung-scientistsclub.com.

- *BrainPOP.* This website specializes in streaming Internet movies to teach a variety of curriculum subjects. The links here are for science-specific subjects, are fairly voluminous, and feature fun, lively characters to help students engage with the material. BrainPOP features trial programs and test subjects to try before you buy. www.brainpopjr.com/science.

- *Home Science Needs.* Tons of science experiment ideas and science supplies and science fair project information are available here. It also offers a free email update with special offers, science projects, and more. This site is geared toward homeschoolers and provides an excellent science resource. 665 Carbon Street, Billings, MT 59102; 800-860-6272; www.hometrainingtools.com.

- *Super Science Fair Projects.* This huge website contains tons of great science project ideas. You needn't wait for a science fair to let your homeschooler run amok with his or her scientific imagination here. There is bound to be something on this website to get just about every type of student excited about science, including complete science fair projects. www.super-science-fair-projects.com.

- *The Teaching Tank* and *Teaching Tank Discovery Books.* The Teaching Tank and the Discovery Books are geared for use by grade levels K–12 and were specifically designed to stress the science skills of observing, measuring, calculating, interpreting data, formulating hypotheses, controlling variables, and experimenting. Using these instructional materials, students, teachers, or both can easily demonstrate scientific principles including seed germination and growth, simple diffusion, evaporation and wind, water turbine, solar heating, and much more, in an exciting and visual way. Captivation, Inc., 153 Regan Lane, Portland, ME 04103; ph. 207-797-0949; fax 207-797-3506; www.tchg.com and www.TeachingTank.com.

- *TOPS Learning Systems.* Treat your family to inventive hands-on science and math with TOPS Learning Systems. Its informative website offers forty-eight sample activities absolutely free—one for each book it has published. Click on titles, listed by grade level, for plenty of informative detail. The index suggests flexible target ages for the materials, pointing out that homeschoolers can often work outside the suggested age ranges. While you are visiting, don't miss the handy Homeschool Tips page for useful feedback from actual users. www.topscience.org.

List 3.6. Foreign Language Learning Resources

As a homeschooler, you will become very aware of the value of learning foreign languages—whether ancient ones like Latin and Greek or the modern, actively used languages like Spanish and French. However, there are two different methods of mastering a language. One is the book method that most of us are familiar with, whereby the student learns the mechanics of the language—the grammar, which includes parts of speech, word endings, genders, agreements, and so on—and then translating from a book. This method provides literate information, so one can possibly read and write the foreign language, but it does not teach one how to speak the language. The other way to learn a language is the way you learn your own native language—by hearing it spoken to you and around you and then joining in! It's called *total immersion,* and it actually teaches you to speak the language, although not how to read or write in it. Both methods are valuable and necessary for one to fully enjoy a language.

Most colleges still require two years of foreign language study for admission, and homeschoolers often enjoy the opportunities to travel and learn about other countries, so knowing at least some of a foreign language through both methods—book and immersion—makes the experience much more valuable and enjoyable.

The following products may use one or both methods.

- *Auralog – Tell Me More Series Language Software* (grades 7 to adult). This software program provides a special version for homeschoolers in three different learning modes as well as a pronunciation aid. With this program you can actually hear what you should sound like and how to pronounce sounds phonetically, rather than having to wait until you are trying to converse with a native speaker of the language! For visual learners, this program demonstrates the positions your mouth should be in when saying certain sounds. Tell Me More also includes exercises and drills you can activate to gain more practice on specific skills you may need work on. In the guided section you can watch digital tours of the land whose language you are studying. 3710 E. University Dr., Ste. 1, Phoenix, AZ 85034; ph. 888-388-3535 or 602-470-0300; fax 602-470-0311; homeschool@auralog.com; www.auralog.com.
- *Rosetta Stone – Dynamic Immersion Technique Software* (grades 7 through adult). This program has been used for a number of years by the CIA and other U.S. government agencies to train their people in foreign languages. Rosetta Stone uses the power and flexibility of the computer to teach both methods. Because computers can generate

sound, Rosetta Stone users can actually hear what the pronunciation should be and develop their "ear" just as they did to learn their own language. The sight capabilities and interaction of the computer make it possible to become literate in the foreign language as well. Rosetta Stone calls this approach "Dynamic Immersion," and it allows the user to learn both aspects of the chosen language with a minimum of tedium and boredom. Rosetta Stone currently offers more than thirty languages. 800-788-0822; www.rosettastone.com.

- *Power-Glide* (grades pre-K–12 and adult). Dr. Robert Blair, eminent language teacher and writer, developed the Power-Glide approach to foreign language learning many years ago. He has had the opportunity to test his theories and practices in the field, teaching many groups of American students a variety of languages. Dr. Blair combined the four prominent theories of language learning from the 1960s to the 1980s. The result was Power-Glide, which has also become one of the most popular and successful language methods available. Currently Power-Glide offers Spanish, French, Latin, and German in a variety of products, including CD-ROMs, books, flash cards, and more. Power-Glide is also an accredited language school through the National Association of Accredited Schools (NAAS), which means that the school can grant credits for its courses. Power-Glide Foreign Language Courses, 1682 West 820 North, Provo, UT 84601; office hours, 8 to 5 Mountain Time; 800-596-0910 or 801-373-3973; www.power-glide.com.

- *Concordia Language Villages (CLV)* (grades 1–12). This novel and unique approach to total immersion of language learning has been around since 1961. At that time a German professor at Concordia College in Moorhead, Minnesota, created a two-week German summer camp for students ages seven through twelve. Since that time the Concordia Villages have grown considerably; in 2005 they offered thirteen languages to nearly 9,500 students between ages seven and eighteen. The concept of a language-immersion camp is very appealing, and students can earn high school credits in twelve of the languages offered at the Villages. The entire approach at CLV—learn and have so much fun that you don't even think you are learning—fits in well with homeschooling. 901 8th Street South, Moorhead, MN 56562; 800-222-4750; clv@cord.edu; www.concordialanguagevillages.com.

- *Pimsleur* (grades 7 to adult). Dr. Paul Pimsleur was controversial in his day, going against the prevailing language-teaching wisdom, but now his method is considered one of the best available. He found that with his method he could teach virtually anyone to speak in thirty minutes per day of application. He did away with quizzes and tedium as well. Pimsleur Direct is now owned by Simon & Schuster and, teamed with the Audiofy company, has developed a memory chip medium for storing the lessons. This makes it possible to take your language lesson along in the car or on the train or plane—virtually anywhere. Pimsleur also offers a wide array of languages, including Irish Gaelic! www.pimsleurdirect.com.

List 3.7. Music Resources

Homeschoolers appreciate the arts and especially music. They realize the importance of learning to play an instrument and to appreciate great music of the past as well as contemporary music. Many of them learn the value of music beginning with church participation and then move into private instrument or voice study as a result. Their parents teach them music history or appreciation or enroll them in classes that do so.

Long before the Mozart Effect was identified, homeschooling families knew that music has a profound effect on children's lives and minds. Here are some very good music instruction programs of varying types—piano, various instruments, rental companies, voice, music history, appreciation, and other skills.

This section includes the following subject areas:

A. Music Instruction Resources – Nonreligious
B. Music Instruction Resources – Religious
C. Instrument Rental and Music Retailers

List 3.7A. Music Instruction Resources – Nonreligious

- *Amadeus Home Music School* (in-home instruction and music therapy). This novel return-to-tradition music instruction company is the brainchild of Michael Lawson, graduate of Juilliard and Northwestern. He hires world-class high-level professional instructors around the country, who will come to your home to teach virtually any instrument, currently including piano, voice, guitar, cello, violin, viola, and saxophone. Amadeus also provides certified music therapists. Contact Amadeus with your location and instruction preferences and they will do the rest. 877-537-7600; www.music-housecalls.com.

- *Piano for Quitters* and *Piano for Life* (DVD/video). These two instruction programs function as parts 1 and 2 in a series designed to teach anyone, with any level of skill or experience, to play piano or electronic keyboard. Using the insights of Franz Liszt and other great teachers, Piano for Life, Inc., has produced a complete six-and-a-half-hour course that anyone can use to learn or teach with. Piano for Life, Inc., P.O. Box 1510, Milton, WA 98354; 888-742-6653 or 253-952-7788; www.justforfunpiano.com.

- *Piano for Preschoolers.* If your young child wants to learn to play the piano but your musical skills or bank account are sorely lacking in substance, Piano for Preschoolers is exactly what you need. Piano for Preschoolers is a fun and educational system that allows children to play songs on their very first try, and it makes it possible for you to successfully teach your preschooler the piano. Founded and owned by a homeschool mom, PFP uses color-coded notes written on a staff, corresponding with a color strip that rests behind the piano keys, so your child makes the easy connection between colors and, ultimately, the more difficult connection of written note with piano key. Piano for Preschoolers, 1035 Sunset Canyon Drive, South Dripping Springs, TX 78620; 866-901-1041; www.pianoforpreschoolers.com.

- *Singing Made Easy* (CD-ROMs and print). This course is the result of more than forty-five years of teaching voice and seven years of thinking and creating custom materials by Marcia McCarry. Ms. McCarry had the aid of Dr. Shinichi Suzuki, founder of the Suzuki Method of teaching instrumental playing, and his wife. Ms. McCarry applied the technique to teaching singing as a natural extension of the method. Her five-level course can train any singer in the comfort of his or her own home. Besides her innovative singing products, Ms. McCarry also offers Acting for Singers and other products. 406-222-6307; www.singingmadeeasy.com.

- *Guitar Lessons Interactive* – Guitar Lessons Online. No matter what style of guitar your child wishes to learn, this website is the place to do it.

With the use of a webcam, the teachers at GLI provide instruction in the complete gamut of musical information: music theory, classical guitar, fingerstyle guitar, jazz guitar, folk guitar, electric guitar, bass guitar, blues guitar, and acoustic guitar. They also offer sheet music, guitars, and accessories of all sorts. Guitar Lessons Interactive, 1162 Sawgrass Dr., Gulf Breeze, FL 32563; 850-934-7135; www.guitarlessonsinteractive.com.

- *Simply Music* (grades 1–7). This program for learning to play piano was founded by an Australian man, Neil Moore, who demonstrated great musical talent as a child. He was very proficient at playing by ear, and as he grew older he increased his natural talent and did not learn to read music until he was in his thirties. Moore feels that people should learn to play music as they learn to talk—long before they can read words—and he developed Simply Music to do just that. Find out more about his approach: P.O. Box 160663, Sacramento, CA 95816; 800-746 7597 (in the USA) or + 1 916 646 0581 (outside the USA); www.simplymusic.net.

- *Let's Sing and Learn: Skill-Building Through Music* (video) (grades 1–8). John Langstaff, the founder of Revels, Inc., in Cambridge, Massachusetts, has taught classroom music for many years. Author of twenty-three children's books and song collections, he hosted the BBC's Schools Television series *Making Music* and was presenter for the NBC-TV series *Children Explore Books*. He has appeared as commentator and soloist in concerts for children with many orchestras, from the New York Philharmonic to the Montreal Symphony. His videos cover such skill development as singing on pitch, rhythm, tone, and dynamics. These are the building blocks for the Let's Sing program. California Revels, 337 17th Street #207, Oakland, CA 94612; 510-452-9334; www.calrevels.org.

- *Rhythm Band Instruments* (RBI). RBI has been providing various simple percussion instruments to homeschoolers for many years. Its maracas, tambourines, triangles, xylophones, and the like have graced many a homeschool group's rhythm bands and provided hours of early musical learning and pleasure. RBI now offers even more resources for families, including instruction videos, books, and a thrift store where it sells slightly blemished or damaged instruments at great discounts. If you have never experienced the fun of a rhythm band, this is a good place to begin! P.O. Box 126, Ft. Worth, TX 76101; 800-424-4724; www.rhythmband.com.

List 3.7B. Music Instruction Resources – Religious

- *Davidsons Music* (grades 5–9). Davidsons Music offers a wide variety of easy-to-play songbooks for Christian piano students. It feels that with its materials one can teach oneself to play without the aid of a teacher. It offers Teach Yourself to Read Music book and cassette packages that cover the basics, plus supplemental books that focus on specific skills, including key signatures, major and minor scales, and more. Davidsons also offers a variety of piano song books and guitar books for actually applying what is learned in the Reading Music section. 6727 Metcalf, Shawnee Mission, KS 66204; ph. 913-262-4982; fax 913-22-2980; www.davidsonsmusic.com.

- *Lester Family Music (Become a Family Choir!)* (grades 3–11). The Lester Family has recorded four educational cassettes that can teach your family or class how to sing in two, three, and four-part harmony. Each recorded song is sung with the soprano, alto, tenor, and bass separately, and then again with all parts sung together. Each child decides which part he or she wants to learn, then listens and memorizes that part. The Lesters' approach is all done by ear without written notation. (Children generally find learning by ear to be very easy.) Once the parts are memorized, the family or class can practice singing the song in harmony without the help of the tape. P.O. Box 203, Joshua Tree, CA 92252; 760-366-1023; info@lesterfamilymusic.com.

- *Pfeiffer House Music* (grades K–6). This website offers complete K–6 Christian music teaching curricula. The company offers a Bible-based perspective, and some of the exercises and tunes contain lines from Scripture. It also provides hymns and booklets and customized accompaniments on MP3s for churches and music majors. www.pfeiffer housemusic.com.

List 3.7C. Instrument Rental and Music Retailers

This section is included because often a family interested in lessons cannot find a satisfactory resource close at hand. These national providers can meet most any instrument need easily and economically.

- *National Educational Music Company (NEMC).* For over fifty years NEMC has been providing high-quality musical instruments for rent or rent-to-own through local music stores and dealers. NEMC provides a complete turnkey program; all the local store owner has to do is sign up with it. NEMC takes care of advertising, rental applications and approval, the instrument inventory, repair, and exchange, if necessary. For young string players, NEMC allows a trade-up feature for transitioning from half-size violin to full-size, without losing any of the rental monies paid. If you have a child who is interested in learning to play an instrument, visit NEMC's website and also talk with your local music store about this rental program. www.nemc.com.
- *Woodwind & Brasswind.* WW & BW is one of the largest music retailers anywhere and especially on the Internet. It carries everything from orchestral instruments to guitar amplifiers. No matter what instrument your children are interested in or what type of music, you can find what they need at WW & BW. The company offers a huge array of accessories and sheet music, too. 800-348-5003; www.wwbw.com.
- *Folk Notes* (dulcimers, banjos, old-time music). If you or your child yearn to play the hammered dulcimer or Irish harp or a join a bluegrass band, Folk Notes will be like heaven. The company carries a broad array of old-time instruments and accessories to make your "mountain music" sessions better. Many homeschooling families appreciate the original sound of Appalachia and can find everything they need right here. 877-273-4999; http://folknotes.com.
- *West Music.* West is a huge one-stop instrument retailer both online and in-house. There are seven locations in Iowa and Illinois, and it also offers its entire stock online. Visit the website for great deals on everything from harmonicas to drums, sheet music to music stands. www.westmusic.com.

List 3.8. Art and Art History

As public schools have been able to devote less and less of their operating budgets to the arts—drawing, painting, art history, music, and drama—families have consistently considered homeschooling as a viable alternative to public school, particularly because the arts are so vital to raising a well-rounded, culturally intelligent child. Studies are regularly demonstrating that children who receive art instruction when young grow up to be more creative and imaginative as adults. As a result of the value homeschooling families tend to give to art, there are many drawing and painting programs available, as well as art history products, that cater to homeschoolers. Each instruction program has a unique character, just as each painter has his or her own character.

This section includes the following subject areas:

A. Art Instruction Resources
B. Art History Instruction Resources
C. Art Supply Resources

List 3.8A. Art Instruction Resources

- *Art Instruction School (AIS)* (grades 8–12). This venerable art school is well known for its famous "Draw Me" ads that have graced magazine pages for over forty years. It is the granddaddy of home instruction art schools and the foremost correspondence art school in the country, with a complete staff of professional, working artists ready to teach you their craft. Take the "Draw Me" challenge and possibly win one of the $14,500 in prizes awarded each month. 3400 Technology Drive, Minneapolis, MN 55418-6000; www.artinstructionschools.com.

- *Atelier Arts Attack* (grades pre-K–11). Atelier offers its art instruction program on video and DVD and is geared specifically for homeschoolers. It is like having an art teacher come to your home, thereby removing stress from the teaching parents who may not be artistically inclined. Atelier offers its program in seven levels and three modules, which can be purchased separately or as a unit, making it very affordable. 4615 Rancho Reposo, Del Mar, CA. 92014; 888-760-ARTS (888-760-2787); www.homeschoolarts.com.

- *Gee Guides* (suitable for grades 2–8). Gee Guides is an excellent, reasonably priced program that provides an enjoyable atmosphere in which to learn about and practice art. Each module of the program provides a wealth of information on the art world, touching on the history of art, great artists, and ideas and techniques of painting or drawing. Included is the Corel digital software, which provides a broad choice of art tools. P.O. Box 3609, Durango, CO 81302; ph. 888-375-0560 or 970-375-0560; fax 970-375-0566; www.geeguides.com.

- *Math Drawings* (grades 4 and up). Although not an art program per se, Math Drawings can provide a playful introduction to drawing and seeing in a more artistic way. Anyone who can draw a straight line with a ruler can draw the pictures in Math Drawings. It can be used to teach math and preliminary art, as well as a few other subjects. The level of the lesson is determined by the age-appropriate level of vocabulary the teacher uses to provide the drawing instructions. Written by Mary Smale, available at www.mathdrawings.com.

- *Arttango.com* (video or online lessons) (grades K–5). Lydia-Kay Blackburn is an art instruction specialist with over twenty years' experience teaching live lessons to public and private elementary school students in the Covington area of Georgia. She has also developed her lessons for homeschoolers on video or delivered online. Each lesson is from seven to fifteen minutes long, thirty lessons per school year, per grade. As each lesson can be viewed again and again, the material can be assimilated easily. 29 Barrett Woods Rd., Covington, GA 30014; 770-787-1890; www.arttango.com.

- *Discovering Great Artists* (pre-K–8). This volume covers eighty artists and provides more than 150 art projects for the student to perform, including drawing, painting, sculpting, and building. Available from Brightring Publishing, P.O. Box 31338, Bellingham, WA 98228; 1-800-480-4278; www.brightring.com.

- *Gordon School of Art* (video instruction) (grades 3–9). Gordon School of Art offers the New Masters program in a video format for home instruction. Founder John Gordon's goal with the New Masters is to communicate his revolutionary system of instruction that enables all students to develop professional-level technical skills in drawing and painting regardless of age or previous skill level. The website features examples of his students' work. 651 Norman Road, Kewaunee, WI 54216; 800-210-1220; john@gordonartinstruction.com; www.newmasters.com.

- *How Great Thou Art* (ages 3 to adult). Mr. Barry Stebbings founded How Great Thou Art in 1991 to fulfill the mission of providing home-schooling families with a high-quality art education in a Christian setting. HGTA currently offers fourteen different curricula for teaching students of all ages in the fundamentals of drawing, painting, color theory, and art appreciation. How Great Thou Art Publications, Box 48, McFarlan, NC 28102; 800-9823729; www.howgreatthouart.com.

- *Teach Art at Home* (CD instruction) (masterpiece art instruction). This program was developed by Ms. Karine Bauch, a graduate of the Fashion Institute of New York, freelance illustrator, and art teacher for ages five and up. Her website offers an extensive array of art instruction products, including watercolor, color theory, and the like. Her progressive level lessons on CD allow the entire family to learn to draw together—even if at different skill levels. www.teachartathome.com.

- *Visual Manna* (Christian art instruction) (grades K–6). Since 1992, this company has offered a wide variety of art instruction materials and art history products as well. One of the featured books, *Art Adventures in Narnia*, will captivate any young artist who dreams of drawing knights, castles, satyrs, and the like. 888-275-7309; www.visualmanna.com.

- *Artistic Pursuits* (K–12). A comprehensive art program designed to involve the student in the creative process while developing observational skills. Each of the books, whether in the K–3 or the 4–12 levels, offers complete overviews and easy-to-understand introductions to the subjects of art and art history. 10142 West 69th Ave., Arvada, CO 80004; 303-467-0504; www.artisticpursuits.com.

List 3.8B. Art History Instruction Resources

- *Artext Prints by Art Extension Press* (grades 5–9). No child's education can be considered complete without a study of the great paintings and painters of Europe and America. To aid in achieving this goal, Art Extension Press offers a line of color art prints in three sizes (3×4, 7×9, or 8×10), which provide a wonderful way to supplement your history, social studies, culture, design, and language studies—as well as pure art study, of course. Artext also has a study book, *Learning More About Pictures,* that coincides with the print sets. P.O. Box 389, Westport, CT 06881; ph. 203-256-9920; fax 203-259-8160; www.artextensionpress.com.

- *Educational Freedom.com* (grades 5–9). This site is a link from the Home Education in Alabama website. It has legal resources and provides a great arts and crafts section, plus nice links to an art history section, a tutorial on 3D drawing, and a link to the Metropolitan Museum of Art. www.educationalfreedom.com.

- *Master's Academy of Fine Arts (MAFA)* (fine arts schools). Although this approach will not suit every homeschooling family's tastes, it is important that readers be aware of the concept. The MAFA currently has fine arts schools located in approximately five states where, one day per week, homeschooled children meet to learn about art history from the ancient civilizations through Medieval/Renaissance, Baroque, Classical, Romantic, and finally the Modern period. If there is not a MAFA school near you, the website, www.mafa.net, offers the interested homeschooling parent (or support group leader) information on how to start one. This is an ingenious idea and demonstrates the resourcefulness homeschooling affords imaginative parents. A professional mom or dad could start a support group–based school to study virtually any topic. Contact Lori Lane, P.O. Box 1953, Loganville, GA 30052; 404-215-8261; www.mafa.net.

- *Pablo's Art Adventures* (grades pre-K–3). This is another ingenious invention of a classroom teacher of many years' experience. Mona Larkins has written and illustrated a series of children's books that tell the story of a little mouse who lives in an art studio; she uses these as a vehicle to teach children the basic concepts of art and art history. Whitehall Publishing; www.pablosartadventures.com.

- *Art History Resources on the Web.* Professor L.C.E. Witcombe of Sweet Briar College in Virginia has an extensive website devoted to everything from prehistoric art to art from numerous countries and cultures. http://witcombe.sbc.edu/ARTHLinks.html.

List 3.8C. Art Supply Resources

There are a large number of national companies that specialize in providing art students and working artists with all of the supplies they need for everything from simple drawing to sculpting. The following are very popular in the homeschooling world.

- *Sax Arts & Crafts.* This company provides a vast array of art and crafts products for drawing in any medium, painting in any medium, sculpting, pottery-making. Via its 345-page catalog, Sax carries brushes, airbrushes, pencils, pens, paper, and other supplies for any art project or necessity. www.saxarts.com.

- *Flax Art & Design.* Despite its whimsical offerings in the Creative Living section of the online store, Flax Art & Design, which began in San Francisco in 1938 as a serious art supply store, continues to serve serious artists of all disciplines, whether working in pastels, watercolors, pen-and-ink, oils, or another medium. And on the whimsical side, Flax searches the world for unusual articles of artistic design—how about a cat-face dinner plate or a color-changing wall clock? To view the extensive catalog, see Flax's website, www.flaxart.com.

- *Dick Blick Art Materials.* Serving artists since 1911, Blick Art Materials currently has thirty stores all over the country and an online store. Besides the standard art supplies, Blick also offers a complete line of anatomical models to draw. There is a two-view human skull, large face parts, adjustable hands, adjustable figures, and much more! The serious still-life art student can gain tremendous knowledge about drawing human figures from these models. See the website for weekly specials. P.O. Box 1267, Galesburg, IL 61402-1267; orders: 800-828-4548 or orders@dickblick.com; products and general information: 800-933-2542 or info@dickblick.com; www.dickblick.com.

- *Educationalfreedom.com.* This site is a link from the Home Education in Alabama website. It has legal resources and provides a great arts and crafts section. Has nice links to an art history section, a tutorial on 3D drawing, and a link to the Metropolitan Museum of Art.

- *TexasArt.com.* With the word "Texas" in the name, you know that this online store is bound to be huge—and it is. The book and video section alone is vast, with great instructional books and videos on every art topic, from oil painting to bookbinding! www.texasart.com.

- *MisterArt.com.* This is another huge arts and crafts supply website. Mister Art carries not only artist needs but also scrapbooking supplies, and there's a Kids' Korner with special items for children. The company offers substantial discounts and has regular specials. 800-721-3015; www.misterart.com.

List 3.9. Civics Resources

Another great value of the Internet is its ability to make important, constant information available to all of us. The topics of civics and citizenship issues are among the most significant we can deal with and teach to our children. Although the following resources are not all homeschool-related per se, they are excellent resources that will provide much help and knowledge.

- *Center on Congress – Indiana University.* All Americans should know the intricacies of the workings of Congress, but how does a parent provide such daunting information to his child? Indiana University provides the answer in a unique and enjoyable fashion—the online Center on Congress. At the Center's website, you can find an incredible number of civics and citizenship resources: How a Member Decides to Vote, Understanding Representative Democracy, The Importance of Civic Participation, and much more. http://congress.indiana.edu.
- *Congress Link.* This is another website dedicated to putting citizens in touch with the work of their elected officials in Washington. It provides a number of subdivisions, such as Congress for Kids and About Government, which offer sublinks with information about all three branches of government, great American documents, voting, icons of American history, and more. www.congresslink.org.
- *Close Up Foundation.* From its website: "The Close Up Foundation is the nation's largest nonprofit (501(c)(3)), nonpartisan citizenship education organization. Since its founding in 1970, Close Up has worked to promote responsible and informed participation in the democratic process through a variety of educational programs." Its twenty-three-page catalog features wall posters of memorials and significant buildings in the nation's capital and a variety of topical and historical books about citizenship, the Constitution, how the government works, and explanations and discussions of important global and domestic issues we all hear about in the daily news. 44 Canal Plaza, Alexandria, VA 22314-1592; 800-256-7387; www.closeup.org.
- *Superintendent of Public Instruction, Washington State – Essential Requirements.* Although this may seem a strange choice for a homeschooling resource, it presents the public school standards for civics and social studies of Washington, and homeschoolers often wish to have some idea of what specific areas their children should be knowledgeable about. Whether the various states' standards are posted for window dressing or actual attainment, they can provide a valuable syllabus outline. www.k12.wa.us.

- *Leadership Initiative.* This website contains many excellent resources and much information to help you teach your child or, if your support group is so inclined, to provide a class in civics. The section on campaign advertising is very impressive, teaching critical thinking as opposed to tactics and empty statements. University of Virginia Center for Politics Youth Leadership Initiative, 2400 Old Ivy Road, P.O. Box 400806, Charlottesville, VA 22904; toll-free 866-514-8389, or 434-243-8468; fax 434-243-8467; ylihelp@virginia.edu; www.youthleadership.net.
- *Alibris Used Books* (high school). Finally, if you search the "Civics" section of this used-book seller, you will find a number of excellent used and affordable books about politics in America and the state of the union for older students. www.alibris.com.

List 3.10. Free Lesson Plan and Unit Study Resources

Teachers and parents continually search for innovative ways to develop lesson plans and unit studies that will provide a comprehensive and relevant education to their students and children.

Creating lesson plans and unit studies, although a rewarding experience, can also be extremely time consuming and can divert valuable time from the act of teaching. Many free lesson plans and unit studies are available to teachers and parents from a variety of quality sources. Most of these resources can be used as stand-alone plans or be customized for personal study preference. Combining resources from various sites gives teachers and parents the opportunity to develop a well-balanced, comprehensive curriculum.

- *Public Broadcasting Service (PBS).* PBS TeacherLine was recently honored as the best educational website designed to provide instructional support for pre-K–12 students, teachers, and administrators. The PBS site offers free lesson plans in areas such as the arts, health and fitness, math, reading and languages, science and technology, and social studies. www.pbs.org/teachers.

- *The Home School Learning Network.* This company is a dynamic online K–12 curriculum service that allows home educators and teachers to access thousands of unit studies, lesson plans, and worksheets. In addition to an affordable subscription-based plan, the company also offers numerous free unit studies and lesson plans, each one containing six to eight lessons, worksheets, answer sheets, and additional resources, covering such topics as Women's History Month: Part 1, American Women; Creative Writing; Ozone and Your Environment; and Understand Volcanoes. Homeschool Learning Network, P.O. Box 957, Kihei, HI 96753; 877-278-5260; info@homeschoollearning.com; www.homeschoollearning.com.

- *Discoveryschool.com.* A wholly owned subsidiary of Discover Communications, Inc, Discoveryschool.com provides innovative teaching materials for teachers, useful and enjoyable resources for students, and smart advice for parents about helping their children enjoy learning and excel in their studies. The site offers a variety of comprehensive lesson plans for elementary, middle, and high school grade levels in all core subjects as well as additional "elective" courses. Each lesson plan includes clearly written objectives, materials lists, procedures, discussion questions, evaluations, suggested readings, and relevant links. Also available are useful teaching tools such as lesson planners and worksheet generators. www.discoveryschool.com.

- *Thelessonplanspage.com.* The Lesson Plans Page is owned and operated by HotChalk, Inc., and was developed to assist educators of all types. Homeschoolers can get lesson plans to use at home, and parents can get ideas for educational activities to use with their children. Over three thousand lesson plans for pre-K–12 and beyond are available for a wide range of subjects including math, science, social studies, technology, and more. HotChalk, Inc., 532 Laguardia Place, #516, New York, NY 10012; 888-468-2336, ext. 508; Webmaster@LessonPlansPage. com; www.lessonplanspage.com.

- *Forlessonplans.com.* This company offers an online directory of free lesson plans for K–12 teachers and can also be accessed by homeschool parents and students, covering such subjects as math, science, social studies, and technology. Lessons consist of age- and grade-appropriate information, materials lists, course objectives, procedures, and tools for evaluating student progress. The site was created by teachers to combine methods and knowledge of teaching solutions and has proven extremely helpful to homeschool educators as well. Lesson plans are thorough and clearly written and can be printed directly from the site. www.forlessonplans.com.

- *Science NetLinks.* The heart of Science NetLinks is the standards-based lesson plans that incorporate skillfully screened Internet resources, and can be selected according to specific benchmarks and grade ranges. Each lesson uses research-based instruction that supports student learning. Lessons are written for teachers, but include student-ready materials that enable students to engage directly in Internet activities. Many lessons include links to relevant reference sites within the body of the lesson. Notably, referenced book pages can be freely downloaded and printed directly from the lessons. www.sciencenetlinks.com.

- *National Geographic Expeditions.* This site offers geographic lesson plans that were written by educators, have been tested in classroom settings, and are fully adaptable to homeschool settings. Together, the lesson plans address all of the U.S. National Geography Standards, the five geography skills, and the main geographic perspectives. The plans include a wide range of teaching strategies with an assessment for each lesson. All lessons are printable and may be adapted based on the needs of students and time constraints. www.nationalgeographic. com/xpeditions/lessons.

- *Center for Distance Learning and Online Learning.* This site provides lists of pre-K–12 websites available for teachers, administrators, parents, and students interested in easy access to useful and appropriate resources provided free of charge to teachers and the general public. It also provides links to hundreds of lesson plans and other material relating to subjects such as math, geography, history, computer technology, language arts, and many more. The site is updated frequently to ensure that resources are current. burton_margie@lacoe.edu; http://teams.lacoe.edu/teachers/index.asp.

- *Middle School Archeology website.* Provides a unit relating to archeology, explaining what it is and isn't, what archeologists strive to achieve in their work, and its value to us. This is not a homeschool site per se, but could be useful to children ages eleven to thirteen or so. www.usd.edu/anth/midarch/arch.htm.

- *Mr. Donn's History* (ages 10–13). This is a great resource for children in this age range. It is packed with enough history and civics material to fill years of study. There are sections on many different African kingdoms and regions, including ancient Egypt, ancient Kush/Nubia, ancient Ghana, Mali, Zimbabwe, and others. There are sections on Rome, Greece, Mesopotamia, China, India, the Celts—and that is just *some* of what is available here. If you have a child who is already a history buff, this website will provide a tremendous amount of pure fun. If your student isn't enthused about history, this might change his or her mind! http://members.aol.com/MrDonnHistory.

- *Britannia History – King Arthur.* At one time or another, most children become enthralled with the "real-life" myth of Arthur and his world. This wonderful website is overflowing with information—maps of Roman roads in Britain, the Celtic tribes in Roman Britain, biographies of Arthur and all of the main characters in his life, and a biography of Geoffrey of Monmouth, Arthur's biographer. Your Anglophile can spend years poring over the information and resources provided here. http://britannia.com/history/arthur.

Part Four

Homeschooling Resources

List 4.1. General Resources

This list provides a broad range of resources for all types of homeschooling philosophies and subjects. Some are specific to a topic; others offer the complete spectrum of study materials and information.

- *American Library Association.* This is the main site of the American Library Association—a worthwhile site in and of itself. In the contents section, look for Great Websites for Kids; here you can explore countless educational websites for students of all ages. www.ala.org.
- *Books 4 Homeschool.* A wonderful resource of book supplies and links specifically directed at homeschoolers. Many of the resources are directed at buying materials, but you'll find a lot of everything here, including a comprehensive list of homeschooling websites and a vast directory of where to obtain specific curriculum materials. www.books4homeschool.com.
- *Eclectic Homeschool Lite.* A free-for-all website with product reviews and articles for beginners to homeschooling. www.eho.org.
- *Homeschool Discount.* An all-encompassing supplies and resources website. Excellent for the diverse variety of materials and especially strong in foreign-language software. www.homeschooldiscount.com.
- *Homeschool Zone.* Informative articles, information about getting started in homeschooling, interviews with leading educators, and simply a fun place to learn about crafts and recipes. www.homeschoolzone.com.
- *Homeschool Reviews.* Want an honest review of a homeschooling product? Homeschoolreviews.com will give you a frank and objective opinion with no strings attached. You will find a multitude of reviews covering everything from educational software to complete curricula. www.homeschoolreviews.com.
- *Homeschooling Friends.* A great general site, Homeschooling Friends offers several articles and a large selection of very interesting links. In addition to all the information included in the site, it offers homeschoolers the capability to arrange educational meetings, classes, and exciting field trips. www.homeschoolingfriends.org.
- *Homeschool Support Network.* The Homeschool Support Network is a great support website for homeschoolers. It offers access to a large online homeschooling support group and article database. www.homeeducator.com.
- *Homeschooling Supply.* Another nice site for finding and buying supplies, with a very helpful browsing tool that allows you to search by subject, grade level, or book publisher. www.homeschoolingsupply.com.
- *Heather's Homeschooling Page.* Heather's Homeschooling Page is an independent site offering a collection of articles in which the author

shares her experience as a homeschooler and also discusses all sorts of topics, from socialization to the philosophy of homeschooling and the importance of learning math. One great thing about this site is its collection of vintage articles discussing classic homeschooling topics such as socialization. www.madrone.com.

- *Teacher Resources.* This site is principally of use for K–12 educators, but contains a wealth of homeschooling and teaching links that are very helpful. www.teacherresources.net.

List 4.2. Religious or Ethnic Homeschooling Resources

List 4.2A. Catholic Homeschool Resources

Catholic homeschoolers have an extensive network of resources and support. Books and other study materials that are acceptable to Catholic families are provided through many different websites and companies. The following are among the best and most useful.

- *Catholic Homeschool Support.* This is an all-encompassing site for Catholic information, including info for new homeschoolers, curriculum resources, and local support groups in all fifty states. www.catholichomeschool.org.
- *Homeschool Goodies.* This site offers state-by-state support information as well as articles, books, news, and links to further information— all of primary interest to Catholic homeschoolers. http://politickles.com/thankevann/homeschoolgoodies/support.php.
- *Homeschool Central – Catholic resources.* This site provides a large amount of resource information subdivided by categories. The Catholic section offers listings of local support groups by state, as well as curriculum and other important information. www.homeschool-central.com/catholic.htm.
- *Cathswap.* This long-time (since 1999) Yahoo! mail group provides a way for Catholic homeschoolers to swap used curriculum with each other. The site guarantees that it monitors the content to filter out anti-Catholic materials and has a sterling track record of satisfaction among its users. http://groups.yahoo.com/group/cathswap.
- *Traditions of Roman Catholic Homes (TORCH).* This is a support site staffed by Catholic laypeople who are in harmony with the church's views on homeschooling and education. Homeschooling parents can form their own TORCH chapters by contacting the main organization at this site. www.catholic-homeschool.com.
- *Catholic Homestudy Network of America (CHSNA).* This organization offers a strong view of parents' sovereign rights and obligations to educate their own children. P.O. Box 2352, Warren, OH 44484; www.chsna.org/index1.htm.
- *Holistic Homeschool Network.* This Catholic support group is based in the South Bay Area of Los Angeles County in Southern California. HHN organizes faith-building activities, which focus on Catholic truths (sacred scripture and tradition). HHN offers a Moms' Bible Study series, boys' and girls' clubs, community service, field trips, traditional Catholic parties, park days, physical fitness challenges, and an academic fair and talent show. Torrance, CA; hhn@altern.org.

List 4.2B. Christian Protestant Homeschool Resources

There are many regional Christian Protestant online support groups. Each one provides a slightly different strong point for advice and support, so please seek them all out to see which one(s) are best for you. Here are a few to get you started:

- *Homeschool Christian.* Offers advice and guidance for new homeschoolers and experienced parents who are looking for fellowship and chat. Besides homeschooling conversation in general, there are also chats about weight loss, finances, and home living. www.homeschoolchristian.com.
- *Christian Homeschool Fellowship on the Web.* Includes a tremendous number of messages and Bible-based advice from homeschoolers all over the country. Another prime example of how the Internet has provided a "global village" closeness to anyone who wishes to participate in it. www.chfweb.net.
- *Christian Homeschooling Moms Webring.* The purpose of this ring is to help homeschooling mothers, both new and experienced, to communicate with each other, offering support and encouragement; to research the Internet for information about homeschooling; and to obtain mentoring and fellowship from each other. http://p.webring. com/hub?ring=chmoring.
- *Christian Homeschoolers.* This site was created and is maintained by the Howards, a Christian homeschooling family in the United States military, currently stationed in Corpus Christi, Texas. They have founded a considerable number of other websites covering a multitude of topics—including military homeschooling, of course—and they offer many products and services of value to homeschooling families. www.christianhomeschoolers.com.
- *Christian Homeschooling US.* This site provides a Homeschool Encouragement Center where you can chat live with a homeschooling mom or dad 24/7. They offer archived articles and current ones pertaining to a number of different homeschooling topics—teen issues, burnout, legal issues, and so on. www.christianhomeschooling.us.
- *What Every Girl Should Know.* WEGSK is for any female from preteen to grandmother and devoted to offering life solutions to Christian women about relationships, inner and outer beauty, virtue and more—all from a Biblical perspective. http://whateverygirl.educationforthesoul.com.

List 4.2C. Islamic Homeschooling Resources

Like many other homeschooling families, Muslim families appreciate the value of protecting their cultural heritage and providing their children with the highest possible quality of academic instruction. These organizations perform excellent service by providing them with the desired resources.

- *Yemen Links.* Networking and resources for Muslim homeschoolers. This site includes much information for the Muslim homeschooler, including lesson plans, other homeschool websites, websites for all Muslim children—homeschooled or not—and much more. http://www.yemenlinks.com.
- *Kinza Academy* (preschool to grade 5). Kinza provides the grammar portion of the trivium well known in the classical education field. The rhetoric and logic portions of the trivium are being developed. Although the Kinza curriculum is secular, it does teach the traditional Islamic sciences and offers religious options to families who wish to educate their children in the Islamic tradition. Kinza Academy, Inc., 231 Market Place, #502, San Ramon, CA 94583; 866-46-KINZA (866-465-4692); 925-242-1414; info@kinzaacademy.com; www.kinzaacademy.com.
- *ArabesQ.* This is a one-stop Islamic resource page for homeschooling families worldwide. One section of the website, the Islamic Academy Online, features an Islamic unit study. Because many great scientists and thinkers have come from the Islamic tradition, ArabesQ uses these ancient resources to teach. The website provides information on all of the software programs the student needs to study online through the Academy as well as details on the custom curriculum approach and all necessary details. www.arabesq.com.
- *MHSNR.* This company provides the most current textbooks and curriculum, "employing the principle of Tarabiyah." Also offers an email loop for announcements of new releases and other important information. www.muslimhomeschool.com.
- *Cynthia Sulaiman's Creative Outlet.* This whimsical and attractive storefront offers Muslim homeschooler coffee mugs, golf shirts, tote bags, and the like, and other items of interest to Muslim shoppers, too. www.cafepress.com/germanrose/343027.

List 4.2D. Jewish Homeschooling Resources

Although there are not huge numbers of Jewish homeschoolers in the United States, the resources serving them are of very high quality.

- *League of Observant Jewish Homeschoolers.* This is a *very* extensive website for Jewish homeschooling networking and information. Besides the Jewish resources, there is a long list of links to other Jewish websites, products, and resources. www.chayas.com/homeschoolindex.htm
- *Torah Educational Software.* This website offers a wide variety of software programs for teaching the Jewish religion and Hebrew, as well as kosher cookbooks, Jewish gift ideas, and other Jewish-related products. www.jewishsoftware.com.
- *Yeshiva Online.* Using the resources of the Internet, this site offers instruction by experienced Rebbeim and Morahs by sight and voice on the Internet in Gemara and Chumash, so "No matter where you are located, there is a Yeshiva to teach your children." 514-733-1077; www.jewishhomeschool.org.
- *Davka Software.* This Jewish software company features products like DavkaWriter, a Hebrew/English word processing program, and DavkaGraphics Collection, a CD-ROM of Jewish clip art. It also features Hebrew-learning software and much more. 8170 N. McCormick Blvd., Suite 111, Skokie, IL 60076; 773-583-2333; New York: 718-928-5521; 800-621-8227; www.davka.com.

List 4.2E. Ethnic Resources

African American Resources

In the 1980s, many African American families felt that because they had fought for a long time to gain entrance into the at-large public school system, they were not anxious to abandon that system for homeschooling. However, more recently many families have realized that it is in their children's best interests to be homeschooled, to ensure high academic achievement and access to the finest products and resources, and also to preserve the family's ethnic culture. As a result, there are now many African American families homeschooling, and their resources are growing all the time.

- *National African American Homeschoolers Alliance (NAHAA).* This is the largest resource for African American homeschoolers in the United States. It is nonsectarian, seeking simply to provide a unity of support, information, and resources for all who are homeschooling African American children or are African American. www.naaha.com.
- *African American Unschooling.* This site provides plenty of information and resources for unschoolers who are also Africentric. There is a teen connection section, a map to aid in meeting other families, a quarterly e-zine, even an Africentric store with unique gifts for homeschoolers. 7549 W. Cactus Rd., Ste. 104-340, Peoria, AZ 85381; 623-205-9883, M–Fri, 10–3 Mountain Standard Time; www.afamunschool.com.
- *African American Homeschoolers Network (AAHN).* Founded in 2002, the organization has grown steadily. It provides resources, support connection, and much information for African American families who are homeschooling or interested in homeschooling. P.O. Box 491253, Atlanta, GA 30349; www.aahnet.org/contact.htm.
- *African American Christian Homeschoolers (AACH).* Provides support and information for all homeschoolers, regardless of race, but seeks to be of service to African American Christian families especially. RR 2 Box 1309, 201 Taylor Road #58, Roland, OK 74954; ph. 866-642-9546; fax 918-427-0263. Contact: Wanda Wilson, 479-522-9265.

Native American Resources

- *Native American Homeschool Association.* The Native American Homeschool Association is affiliated with Native American Home Education (NAHE) and is working on its own curriculum guidelines, to as many concerns of education as possible, including the following:
  1. A curriculum based on combining state requirements with Native American areas of -09study.
  2. A curriculum that can be used as a guideline for tribes and tribal organizations in which several or many students are involved. This

program of study would reflect the mandates of the tribe rather than the state.

3. A curriculum that doesn't even take state mandates into consideration. Misty Dawn Thomas, director, P.O. Box 979, Fries, VA 24330; www.mo-biz.com/~mvha/NativeAmericanHomeschoolers.html.

- *Native American Home Education (NAHE).* NAHE is an organization for Native American homeschooling families across North America, created by a Cherokee-Catawba homeschooling mother of three. NAHE headquarters is in the Blue Ridge Mountains of North Carolina. It is currently seeking people to begin chapters of NAHE across the United States. Membership in the NAHE is free. To start a chapter in your state or to join NAHE in North Carolina, and for more information, contact Sharyn Robbins-Kennedy, president and founder, P.O. Box 464, Bostic, NC 28018; Nuwahti@yahoo.com; www.geocities.com/nuwahti/NAHE.html.

- *Native American Homeschoolers Yahoo! Group.* A support and mailing group for those homeschooling or unschooling with a Native American background or ancestry who are trying to teach without Christian influence. In early February 2007 this group had new activity and growth. Keywords: Native American, Indian, homeschool, unschool, indigenous, United States, Canada, Mexico. http://groups.yahoo.com/group/NAHomeschoolers.

- *Abaetern Academy.* This online school uses the Coursework for American Indian and Rural Nascent (CAIRN) project curriculum, which is funded by the U.S. government and available to those outside of those groups. The school incorporates American Indian culture and themes in every course offered. Cultural content is evaluated and approved by tribal consultants. Not all of the high school diploma work is done on the computer. Students must complete community-based assignments and a senior project. http://www.abaetern.com.

Pagan Resources

The growth of paganism or practitioners of the Old Religion has led to a commensurate growth in its homeschooling activity. Among the best are these three:

- *www.tarotreadings.net/paganhs.html.* Reverend Silver Darksky's site has a long list of reasons to homeschool and a number of useful links to diverse resources, such as museums, science sites, math pages, and the Wonders of the Ancient World.

- *www.kristinmadden.com.* This is the website for Kristin Madden, a shaman with thirty-five years' experience in the shamanistic and natural healing arts, trained environmentalist and biologist, author of numerous books, and homeschooling mom to boot! One of Kristin's books is *Pagan Homeschooling,* published by Spilled Candy and available on www.alibris.com.

- *Circle Magick Homeschooling — www.geocities.com/moonedreamer/moonedreamer1.html.* This site belongs to MooneDreamer, who home-schools her three daughters in North Carolina. She includes many interesting articles here, and her other website, www.geocities.com/sablehs, contains many useful homeschooling links and information.

List 4.3. Curricula Types

A boxed curriculum is literally a standardized set of products packed in a box. It offers the same texts, workbooks, teacher's manual, and so on, in every box, for each grade. The provider typically offers teacher assistance in grading, guidance, and record-keeping.

A customized curriculum is usually offered by a person who has experience in homeschooling—possibly a former schoolteacher turned homeschooling parent—who provides advice and guidance regarding various aspects of choosing materials, such as a child's learning style, particular challenges, and so on. These providers may not offer the further lesson-by-lesson guidance, grading, and record-keeping that may be provided for a boxed curriculum, so be sure to inquire at the outset.

This section includes the following subject areas:

A. Boxed Curricula – Religious

B. Boxed Curricula and Correspondence Schools – Nonreligious

C. Custom Curricula – Religious

D. Custom Curricula – Nonreligious

List 4.3A. Boxed Curricula – Religious

Catholic

- *Catholic Heritage Curricula* (CHC). Offers a complete K–12 curriculum but not one that is prepackaged. Instead, it allows as much individual "fit" as is sensible to maintain student interest and still offer a complete education. Lesson plans and all books and materials are included. CHC provides sound Catholic teaching as well as nonreligious academic subjects and even offers instructional materials for First Communion. CHC's website also includes an online support feature, "Mom to Mom," to help guide parents in their homeschooling adventure. www.chcweb.com/catalog/index.html.

- *Kolbe Academy.* This bricks-and-mortar school in Napa, California, also provides a complete boxed curriculum for homeschooling students. The curriculum is classically based, including Latin and Greek, and uses the Great Books of the Western world rather than textbooks. Kolbe's teaching plan centers around the Catholic Church and its place in history—the period before the existence of the Church for the ancient world material, post-Church for the Medieval period and somewhat later. Homeschool, 2501, Oak St., Napa, CA 94559; 707-255-6499; Day School, 707-256-4306; homeinfo@kolbe.org; www.kolbe.org.

- *Seton Home Study.* This Catholic company publishes its own workbooks and textbooks for Catholic homeschoolers grades K–12. The curriculum is individualized, so students with certain special needs can use Seton's materials successfully. Seton also offers a number of online high school courses, with more being added. 1350 Progress Drive, Front Royal, VA 22630; ph. 540-636-9990, fax 540-636-1602; info@setonhome.org; www.setonhome.org/curriculum/default.php.

Mormon

- *Brigham Young University Independent Study* (high school). BYU Distance Learning Division offers over six hundred university, high school, and personal enrichment courses, both online and traditional correspondence courses. It is accredited by the Northwest Commission on Colleges and Universities, and the Independent Study High School Program is accredited by the Northwest Association of Accredited Schools (NAAS). http://ce.byu.edu/is/site.

Islamic

- *Kinza Academy* (presently offers preschool to grade 5, but plans to add grades in the future). Kinza Academy currently offers a secular curriculum, but it also teaches the traditional Islamic sciences and offers

Islamic religious options to families who wish to educate their children in the Islamic tradition. Kinza Academy, Inc., 231 Market Place, #502, San Ramon, CA 94583; 866-46-KINZA (866-465-4692); 925-242-1414; info@kinzaacademy.com; www.kinzaacademy.com.

Protestant Christian

- *Landmark Freedom Baptist Curriculum* (Baptist). Landmark Freedom Baptist Church in Florida provides this complete Bible-based curriculum for Baptists. They offer all of the core subjects, plus Bible Study using the King James version and Soul Winning. They also offer a K–5 program separately. 2222 E. Hinson Ave., Haines City, FL 33844; 800-700-LFBC; LFBC@Juno.com; www.landmarkbaptistchurch.org/lfbc.
- *Accelerated Christian Education (ACE)* and *School of Tomorrow*. This company provides curriculum for the Lighthouse Christian Academy and other Christian schools, as well as to individual homeschooling families. Homeschoolers can, if they wish, take care of record-keeping, grading, and so forth themselves by following the Parent Orientation Guide provided by ACE. The company writes and publishes all of its own books and video presentations and provides a grade-by-grade curriculum-in-a-box for K–12. P.O. Box 4700, Seminole, FL 33775; 727-319-0700; Info@ACEministries.com; www.schooloftomorrow.com.
- *A Beka Books* and *A Beka Academy*. This Christian company provides both a complete boxed curriculum for K–8, the Child and Parent Kit, and a complete correspondence course in the form of (leased) DVD classes through the A Beka Academy for grades K–12. In the Academy format, which is fully accredited, A Beka provides everything a regular school does, including the textbooks, lesson plans, progress reports, and so on. The student completes the work and sends it to A Beka for grading and recording. The Academy also keeps and provides transcripts of the student's work and an annual graduation ceremony. Box 19100, Pensacola, FL 32523-9100; 877-223-5226; www.abeka.com.
- *Alpha Omega Publications.* Alpha Omega provides a complete Protestant Christian-based curriculum, LIFEPAC, for K–12 that includes diagnostic tests, self-tests, and teacher checkpoints that help parents track the progress and academic development of their children as they work through the LIFEPAC lessons. Alpha Omega offers the Power-Glide Foreign Language courses developed by Dr. Robert Blair, an internationally recognized language expert. Also offered is the Weaver Curriculum, which is completely Bible-based, for grades K–12. 300 North McKemy Ave., Chandler, AZ 85226; ph. 602-438-2717, fax 480-940-3730; adavis2@aop.com; www.aop.com.

- *Sonlight Curriculum, Ltd.* Sonlight offers a three-size, four- or five-day curriculum that requires only a few minutes per day of teacher preparation, but is hands-on in its full execution. It also bases its curriculum on literature rather than textbooks. Well-written books—"real" books, as some people call them—fill in historical events with real-life people. They instill in children actual concepts and ideas, paving the way for actual thought to take place when the child reaches the appropriate age. Sonlight provides the books, which come from a variety of sources. 8042 South Grant Way, Littleton, CO 80122-2705; 303-730-6292; www.sonlight.com.

- *Robinson Self-Teaching Curriculum* (K–12) (CD-ROM). Dr. Art Robinson homeschooled his six children alone, following the sudden demise of his wife. He had to resort to having the children virtually teach themselves under his direction, as he had to continue working to earn a living. He compiled the Robinson Curriculum, which is on twenty-two CD-ROMs. The math is a special self-teaching method developed by Dr. Robinson. Many users of the curriculum complete math through calculus by age sixteen. It is a "no-nonsense" approach, strong on reasoning and critical thinking. Oregon Institute of Science, P.O. Box 1279, Cave Junction, OR 97523; robinsoncurriculum@yahoo.com; www.robinsoncurriculum.com.

- *Hewitt Homeschool Resources.* This company offers both Christian and secular books in its curriculum. They provide guidance about what is best for your child and for grades 7 through 12 and offer more oversight for those who wish it. They offer graduation, transcripts, and other services, as well. This company has a very broad and flexible view—an excellent fit for homeschoolers in general. P.O. Box 9, 2103 B St., Washougal, WA 98671; 369-835-8708; www.hewitthomeschooling.com.

List 4.3B. Boxed Curricula and Correspondence Schools – Nonreligious

- *Calvert School* (K–12). Calvert has been a bricks-and-mortar day school in Baltimore for over 125 years. During that time, it has offered one of the most popular correspondence courses available. Each grade is complete with all of the materials specified in the Teacher's Manual, including pencils, rulers, notebooks—everything necessary to complete the entire grade. Calvert also offers two options, of complete teacher assistance or not, for two different prices. 105 Tuscany Road, Baltimore, MD 21210; 888-487-4652 or 410-243-6054; admissions@calvertschool .org for catalog; www.calvertschool.org.

- *American School* (high school). The American School has been providing correspondence education for over one hundred years. It offers a complete four-year diploma program and is accredited by the NCA and CITA accrediting agencies. It offers year-round enrollment and teacher support. The school has a completely flexible approach, so it allows students to work at their own pace, but also offers accelerated learning to anyone who desires it. 2200 E. 170th St., Lansing, IL 60438; 708-418-23800; www.americanschoolofcorr.com.

- *Cotton's Journey* (grades 1–8). This is a unique unit study approach using cotton as its basis. Because this crop has had such an impact on the culture and history of America, it stands to reason that its study would prove insightful. The creators have developed lessons with teacher's guides in book and CD-ROM format that teach math, reading, writing, science,and so on, learning about, and working with, cotton. They have created some of the materials themselves, and even what they have not developed is available through their website. Parents can use this as the primary curriculum resource or as a supplementary program. P.O. Box 55, Tranquillity, CA 93668; 800-698-1888; www.cottonsjourney.com.

- *Kendall/Hunt Publishing Company*. K–12 curricula provide everything you need to homeschool your child successfully. The company provides lessons, supplemental materials, planning aids, assessments, and more. There is also a gifted education program. 800-770-3544; www.kendallhunt.com/homeschool.

List 4.3C. Custom Curricula – Religious

- *The Dow's Schoolroom* (Christian). Diana Dow is the homeschooling mom of six children. She has been homeschooling since 1991 and has been operating Dow's Schoolroom since 1996 as a hub of curriculum information and materials. She provides advice and offers the recommended products for sale as well. Her expertise in the field of homeschooling is helpful, especially to parents new to homeschooling. P.O. Box 560, Huntington, TX 75949; 866-788-0862 or 936-422-4623; www.thedowsschoolroom.com.

- *Rod & Staff Publishers* (Christian). This company provides a complete Bible-based textbook curriculum for grades 1–8 and partial curriculum for grades 9 and 10. Its products are of the highest academic and Christian quality, written from a conservative Mennonite point of view. The company itself does not have a website, but a search of the Internet will produce other online providers. However, it offers a free catalog of its fine materials. P.O. Box 3, Crockett, KY 41413-0003; ph. 606-522-4348; fax 800-643-1244.

- *Drills, Skills & More* (Christian). This company is owned by the Wilder family, homeschooling veterans of over eleven years' experience. Besides their online store, the Wilders have a bricks-and-mortar store in San Antonio, Texas. The provide products for custom curriculum building as well as unit study approaches. 7002 Forest Crest North, San Antonio, TX 78240; 800-352-2347 or 210-680-5388; www.drills-skills.com.

List 4.3D. Custom Curricula – Nonreligious

- *Educator's Exchange.* This company has a bricks-and-mortar store in Richmond, Virginia, as well as the online version, where it offers used curriculum, books, and study materials from a vast array of publishers and a huge list of topics. 10755 Midlothian Turnpike, Richmond, VA 23235; 888-257-4159; www.edexbooks.com.

- *Design-a-Study (DAS).* Kathryn Stout began her company after eight years of teaching in public school. She was homeschooling her two small children and developed a custom curriculum for them. Other parents began to ask her advice, and ultimately she started DAS to provide them with guidance and materials. Ms. Stout provides spelling, math, history, movies as literature, and all other core topics and some unit studies as well. Design-a-Study, 408 Victoria Ave., Wilmington, DE 19804-2124; 800-965-2719 or 302-998-3889; www.designastudy.com.

List 4.4. Homeschooling with Nonelectric Games

Often the best way to learn and review any material is by making it fun. An awareness of learning through enjoyable board games is one of the great pleasures of homeschooling. When the entire family can play together, this makes it even better for the learners. Because a large number of homeschooling families limit or eliminate the playing of computer-based electronic games and television watching, there is a constant interest in board games. Luckily, there are many, many excellent nonelectric educational games available—some that homeschoolers have enjoyed for years, others that are brand new—with more being created all the time. Here are a few of the best that we know of:

- *Elemento* (ages ten to adult, two to six players). This is an ingenious game based on the periodic table of elements. It is set up like a quasi-Monopoly board with the elements in place of properties. Players wend their way through the elements, buying them with proton or neutron cards. A great way to memorize the periodic table for chemistry and other science applications. Lewis Educational Games, Box 727, Goddard, KS 67052; 800-557-8777; www.members.aol.com/dickwlewis.
- *Karmel Games – Language Skills.* Karmel produces two board games that encourage development of language skills. Anagramania is for two to six players and aids in reading, semantic recognition, and procedural logic. Players race against each other and must unlock anagrams as clues to move ahead. Nymble requires players to find as many word pairs as possible from three different categories—synonyms, antonyms, and homonyms. Playing these two games will provide hours of fun and language skill improvement for your children. Karmel has other intelligent games as well. 501-I S. Reino Rd., #228, Thousand Oaks, CA 91320; 866-350-4320; www.karmelgames.com.
- *Uncle Lester's Word Games* (four editions – Bible, Family, Student [grades 1–8], Secular). These multilayered games were developed by a family and are suitable for ages seven through adult, as each one has three different levels of difficulty per question. The player rolls the dice and the number determines the degree of difficulty, depending on the player's age group. Hovda Game Services, Inc., 3821 E. State St. #124, Rockford, IL; 815-226-0327; www.hovdagame.com.
- *Wildcraft! – The Medicinal and Edible Herb Game.* Know which plants around you are edible or medicinal. Great for survival situations. The same company also makes a home study course about using herbs for natural care. This is a great practical education to give to your

entire family—natural first aid! Learning Herbs.com, P.O. Box 1174, Carnation, WA 98014; 206-963-4880; www.learningherbs.com.

- *The Comprehension Zone—Rocket Rap.* This game builds reading and auditory comprehension while using science and historical figures as the subject matter. It is multiage, too—children in grades 2 and 3 learn about space, grades 4 through 6 learn about American biographies, and grades 7 through 12 learn about international biographies—and all three levels can play at the same time. Bonnie Terry Learning, 238 Poet Smith Dr., Auburn, CA 95603; 530-888-7160; www.bonnieterrylearning.com.

- *Pick Two* (ages eight to adult, three to six players; available in English, Spanish, or French). In this game, each player builds a personal cross-word puzzle as fast as possible, using letter tiles. The first player to do so yells "Pick two!"; then everyone, including the caller, picks up two more tiles that must be added immediately to the crossword. Players can rearrange their tiles to change the crossword. When the pile of tiles is gone, the first player finished wins. Over time, playing this game will create practice spelling and increase vocabulary. Tah Dah, Inc.; 815-624-8337; www.discovergames.com.

- *Sentence Says* (ages seven to adult). This unique game provides a review and supplemental study of sentence structure, diagramming, and parts of speech, which ultimately enhance communication skills. Players roll dice to see how many letter cards they obtain and how much time they will have to create a sentence from them. Opponents can steal your sentence and its points, however. The first player to reach 100 points wins. MarBan, Inc., 2633 Lincoln Blvd. #258, Santa Monica, CA 90405; 310-827-4546; www.sentencesays.com/prdt-sent-ss.htm.

- *Create-a-Story – The Creative Writing Game* (ages ten and up). This one-of-a-kind game was developed by two educational therapists and teaches players how to develop their writing skills. Players collect story elements from the game board, create an outline with them, and then write their story. The game is noncompetitive, focusing more on writing than on beating others, and it is designed so that everyone who achieves a certain number of points wins—which can be every player! Pro Ed Inc., 8700 Shoal Creek Blvd., Austin, TX 78757-6897; 800-897-3202; www.proedinc.com.

- *Educational Learning Games (EL Games)* (all categories). This is a great site for learning games of all sorts. It features a wide variety of language arts games, covering grammar, phonics, reading, spelling, and vocabulary. It offers science games, including human body and anatomy games; Skeleton Bingo; The Way Things Work (from the hit video series);

Bioviva, which addresses nature and the environment; the Science of Special Effects Kit; and much more! EL also carries many Mensa "mind" games, which have been tested by and have won the approval of the Mensa association. 727-786-4850; www.educationallearninggames.com.

- *JAX Games, Ltd.* (strategy and number skills). This company specializes in standard fun games, rather than educational fun games, but these board games are still better for an evening's entertainment than watching television or playing electronic games. Many of these games offer quick-thinking, strategizing, or number skills development. 763-449-9699; www.jaxgames.com.

- *On the Spot Games* (social interaction). Rob Mathewson, owner of On the Spot, developed his games as a way for families to spend more time together interacting instead of staring at the television. One of his games for age five and older is a statement completion game, Did Ya Know? Players complete statements such as "The best candy in the world is . . ." Players can trade assignments and retell the completion provided. All of the games provide fun and laughter possibilities galore. 5518 6th Ave. NW, Seattle, WA 98107; 206-396-0049; www.funonthespot.com.

- *SET, the Matching Symbol Card Game* (brain function). This unique symbolic card game is the brainchild of Marcia Falco, who developed it from a scientific experiment she directed. SET consists of a deck of symbol cards with three basic shapes, three fill patterns, and three colors. The object of the game is to match up as many of the varied combinations as possible. The person with the most sets wins the hand. SET also makes Quiddler, the next entry. SET Enterprises, Inc., 16537 E. Laser Dr., Suite 6, Fountain Hills, AZ 85268; 800-351-7765 or 480-837-3628; www.setgame.com.

- *Quiddler* (spelling and vocabulary). This card game enables you to practice spelling and vocabulary with your student. Quiddler players must combine the entire hand into words, trying to achieve the highest point values. There are different rounds to be played, each with ascending numbers of cards, from three to ten. Made by SET Enterprises, Inc. (see preceding entry).

- *Ampersand Press* (nature and earth science). The board games of Ampersand Press are known for their beautiful artwork gracing both boards and cards, as well as intelligent and significant subject matters that teach nature in a very enjoyable setting. These excellent additions to your homeschool supplementary curricula will provide hours of quiet fun and learning for years to come. 750 Lake St., Port Townsend, WA 98368; 800-624-4263 or 360-379-5187; www.ampersandpress.com.

List 4.5. Audio Learning Resources

Listening to tapes (and, more recently, CDs) has always been a favorite among homeschooling families. Because they usually subscribe to the belief that learning is not an on or off proposition, they take advantage of long car trips to listen to a great storyteller like Jim Weiss or a spellbinding edition of *Boomerang!* The material available on CD is growing constantly. Here are just a few resources for your consideration:

- *Boomerang! The Kids' Audio Magazine. Boomerang!* is a unique way to help your students learn about history, great biographies, and current events and use their imagination as they listen to the cast of *Boomerang!* (all but one or two are kids) as they present their individual ten- to twenty-minute segments of this high-quality audio magazine. Like old-time radio about new-time things! Each cassette or CD is seventy minutes. See the website for some free downloads. P.O. Box 261, La Honda, CA 94020; 800-333-7858; boomerang@boomkids.com; www.boomkids.com.
- *Audio Memory.* Owned by a homeschooling mom, the company's motto is "You never forget what you sing." It is based on the premise that singing certain pieces of information to a melody is the best way to learn and remember them. The company offers a huge variety of titles with cassettes or CDs and booklets to provide hours of entertaining memory work for your student. 501 Cliff Drive, Newport Beach, CA 92663; 800-365-SING; www.audiomemory.com.
- *Sing N' Learn* (Christian). This company, owned by a homeschooling family, offers a wide assortment of titles including Worship Guitar songbooks and other church music, as well as educational products. 2626 Club Meadow Dr., Garland, TX 75043; 800-460-1973 or 972-278-1973.
- *Majesty Music* (Christian). Majesty specializes in sacred music you can trust. One of its mainstays is a novel series of children's CDs centered around the adventures of Patch the Pirate. The songs, all written by Ron Hamilton, are wholesome, humorous, and imaginative. The Patch CDs are enjoyable and can impart life values as well. 800-334-1071 or 864-242-6722; www.majestymusic.com.
- *Greathall Productions.* Jim Weiss is a master storyteller and writer and editor of others' writings. He can make any story fresh and intelligent, finding the nuances to enthrall and stimulate the mind's eye. Students enjoy learning about Greek mythology or Irish tales, Shakespeare or Sherlock Holmes through the melodious voice of this great artist. P.O. Box 5061, Charlottesville, VA 22905; 800-477-6234; www.greathall.com.

List 4.6. Special Needs Resources

There are a number of providers for children with all sorts of special needs from ADHD to autism and dyslexia. Here are some of the varied resources available:

- *Bridgeway Academy Online School* (K–12). This is not exclusively a special needs school. It is a regular K–12, fully accredited, online school providing complete curriculum and enrollment for regular students. However, it also offers knowledge and experience with slow learners and those with various learning disabilities such as ADHD, dyslexia, and dysnomia. Bridgeway Home School Academy, 334 Second St., Catasauqua, PA 18032; 800-863-1474; www.homeschoolacademy.com.
- *Bayshore Learning and Bayshore Private ISP* (K–12). Lenore Hays and her husband, homeschooling parents of a special needs child, have operated Bayshore Private ISP since 1992. It is licensed in California only, but anyone with a special needs child can visit its website for considerable information and resources. P.O. Box 13038, Long Beach, CA 90803; www.bayshoreeducational.com.
- *Homeschooling Special Needs (HSSN)*. This website is the portal for a small group of families homeschooling special needs children. It contains curriculum, medical information, learning resources, and links of all sorts. http://home.att.net/~MikeJaqua/special/frames/.
- *At Our Own Pace*. This special needs homeschooling newsletter is free; however, donations are always welcomed. Jean Kulczyk, 102 Willow Drive, Waukegan, IL 60087; yukko5@aol.com.
- *National Association for Child Development (NACD)*. This organization provides evaluations and specialized programs and support to parents for their special needs children. They provide regular reviews of progress, advice, and counseling. They have local chapters all over the country and some international locales, too. 549 25th Street, Ogden, UT 84401-2422; ph. 801-621-8606; fax 801-621-8389; info@nacd.org; www.nacd.org.
- *National Challenged Homeschoolers Associated Network (NATHHAN)*. This is a resource for Christian homeschooling families with special needs children. It offers a wide assortment of resources and support services. 208-267-6246; nathanews@aol.com; www.nathhan.com.

List 4.7. Charter Schools and Independent Study Programs (ISPs)

The most dramatic change in homeschooling in recent years is the charter school movement. Chartering allows public school districts to add on a "homeschooling" division, with a separate budget and separate staff. The parents teach their children at home, just as traditional homeschoolers do, but they meet weekly, biweekly, or monthly with a teacher, usually at a local school, to discuss the student's progress and allow for teacher review of assigned work and assignment of new work. This works very well for many families, and it gives school districts an intelligent solution to overcrowding and the need for new classrooms or teachers.

One potential drawback—and an important one to consider—is that in some states, enrollment in a charter school program places the child in the same category as a public school child, so that rules such as those for attendance are applicable. For parents who do not mind being chained to the public school calendar, this is probably not a problem, but some families, especially if self-employed, enjoy the autonomy of time that homeschooling affords them; for example, if a special extended field trip (vacation) is coming up, the child can double up on his studying or can take his lessons with him on the road. The learning atmosphere is relaxed and pleasurable. If the family is instead subject to the school calendar and requirements, they may lose a certain amount of freedom and the relaxation of homeschooling.

Each state has its own charter school program; just a few are listed here to provide some seed ideas. Please look into your own state's policies and see what is available.

- *www.uscharterschools.org.* This is a one-stop website for charter school information connected to school districts. It has data relating to the general thinking behind charter schools and state charter school guidelines and laws.

In addition to the public school charter schools, which are part of the local school district, there are privately owned companies that contract with school districts or state departments of education to administer and manage the charter school program. These companies are not in every state. The following are in that category:

- *Connections Academy* (K–12). This company obtains funding from the governmental agencies it contracts with, so it offers its services to families at no charge. It provides core subject matter to students in a full package of materials necessary to complete the school year's work. The instructor works with the parent or guardian in evaluation, review, and assigning and grading of work. Corporate office: 1000 Lancaster St., 6th Flr., Baltimore, MD 21202; ph. 800-382-6010 or 410-843-6010; fax 410-843-6262; info@connectionsacademy.com; www.connectionsacademy.com.

- *K–12 Virtual Academy.* This company provides core subject curriculum and all materials necessary for coursework completion, guidance, evaluation, testing, and grading. What it offers—either a complete virtual academy or supplemental work—varies by state. You can check your state's offerings on its website. Corporate office: K12, Inc., 2300 Corporate Park Dr., Herndon, VA 20171; sales and information, 866-512-2273; www.k12.com.
- *Harvest Prep Virtual Academy* (Christian, grades 3–12). This Christian online, tuition-charging school is available to anyone who lives more than fifty miles from Canal Winchester, Ohio. Locals are encouraged to enroll in the bricks-and-mortar Harvest Prep Academy. This school provides a college prep curriculum, but parents should check for individual school requirements. Testing is also based on the state of residence, so inquire at the outset about this. Harvest Prep Virtual Academy, An Educational Outreach of World Harvest Church, P.O. Box 32903, Columbus, OH 43232-9825; 800-969-4782; info@harvestprepva.org; www.harvestprepva.org.

Independent study programs (ISPs) are usually privately owned companies that usually provide local programs. Some major ones that are national in scope are listed here.

- *Indiana University Independent Study Program* (high school and college). Indiana University has been offering distance learning since 1925 and has added the online choices to its already proven correspondence division. Your student can earn an Indiana U. high school diploma or earn dual credits for high school or college in this self-paced environment. Continuous enrollment and single-course options make it very attractive to homeschooling families nationwide. 800-334-1011; http://scs.indiana.edu/guest/link.html.
- *North Dakota Division of Independent Study* (grades 4–12). This ISP is operated by the state of North Dakota and is fully accredited by the NCAC CASI. It offers a wide variety of courses and programs for homeschoolers—over 180 print and online—as well as granting a high school diploma for those who qualify. P.O. Box 5036, Fargo, ND 58105-5036; 701-231-6000; ndis.enroll@sendit.nodak.edu; www.NDISonline.org.

- *University of Nebraska Independent Study High School.* U of Neb offers advanced placement (AP) courses as well as a complete college prep program and a full diploma program. Continuous enrollment, fully accredited. 866-700-4747; nebraskahs.unl.edu.
- *The Learning Springs.* This program offers over one hundred complete courses as well as supplemental courses for students engaged in another program. P.O. Box 907, Ojai, CA 93024; 800-324-3390; info@learningsprings.com; www.learningsprings.com.
- *Boston School.* Educator John Boston founded his ISP in 1980. Families enroll in his school, which is a fully accredited alternative school, and the school provides all support services, including record-keeping, guidance, and so on. Member families are provided the course suggestions and then are free to obtain materials from whatever sources they wish. P.O. Box 708, Joshua Tree, CA 92252; 760-366-8658; info@bostonschool.org; www.bostonschool.org.
- *University of Mississippi Independent Study High School.* This university offers correspondence and online courses—over 120 in all. Online includes English 9, biology, geography, pre-algebra, and algebra. Visit the website for complete details. rsbeebe@olemiss.edu; www.outreach. oldemiss.edu/youth/indstudy_highschool.
- *CALCampus* (high school and college). This pioneer resource has been offering courses since 1986 and on the Internet since 1995. It has a complete curriculum of courses, including English as a Second Language for non-native speakers. See the complete online catalog. P.O. Box 132, Rindge, NH 03461; 603-899-2388; director@calcampus. com; www.calcampus.com.
- *Griggs University & International Academy* (pre-K to university, Christian). Griggs was formerly known as Home Study International, a widely respected provider of distance learning to homeschoolers. It has expanded its scope to include from pre-K to a complete university curriculum. GU offers two programs for elementary school students—accredited (by the state of Maryland) and nonaccredited, which consists of the books and materials, but no report cards or accreditation. 12501 Old Columbia Pike, Silver Spring, MD 20904; 800-782-4769; www.hsi.edu.
- *University of Oklahoma Independent Learning High School.* U of OK allows for continuous enrollment, self-paced study, self-scheduled testing, and online or correspondence course format. Students can take high school and college courses. 1700 Asp Ave., Norman, OK 73072; 800-522-0772, ext. 4414, or 405-325-4414; www.occe.ou.edu/outreach.

List 4.8. Online Schools – K–12 and High School

These resources are not only for homeschooled children, unless this is specifically noted. However, as the full-time students will be homeschooled, they form the majority of the online enrollment. (Please see List 5.4 for a separate list of online universities.)

- *Ed Anywhere* (middle and high school). This is an excellent online school, run by a man with vision and intelligence, Philip Singh, who sees every student as a success and understands that the academic program should be made to fit the student, not the student to fit the program. EA also provides tutorial support for the parents of enrolled homeschooling students. 877-4ED-0805 (877-433-0805); www.edanywhere.com.
- *Oak Meadow*. This is one of the oldest and most popular schools serving homeschoolers; it has been doing so since 1975. Fully accredited. Online and printed K–12 curriculum, developed by Oak Meadow, is available, as well as software training courses and certifications. P.O. Box 1346, Brattleboro, VT 05302; 802-251-7250; www.oakmeadow.com.
- *University of Texas (High School)*. Since 1998, the UT high school program has been instructing high school students in Texas and elsewhere via DVD and online courses. The program is fully accredited, and when a student completes the entire program, it satisfies the Texas requirements for receipt of a full diploma, just as the bricks-and-mortar high schools do. The UT program allows for flexibility and self-paced work within certain time frames. Dr. Amy Pro; 512-471-1838; apro@mail.utexas.edu; www.utk16.org/uths.
- *Excel High School* (and middle school). This innovative institution provides a complete online grade 6–12 (high school) diploma program as well as makeup high school classes that are accepted by most high schools in the nation. The program is flexible and accommodating to the student's specific needs. 4445 W. 77th St., Ste. 209, Minneapolis, MN 55435; 800-620-3844; www.excelhighschool.com.
- *University of Miami (FL) Online High School*. The U of M offers continuous enrollment with full-time, part-time, or summer school; AP; honors; regular; and elective courses. It also offers college advisers who can help your student plan ahead. 877-871-8163 or 305-689-8647; info@umohs.org; www.umohs.org.
- *American Academy K–12* (Christian). This is the online wing of a correspondence school of long standing, based in Oklahoma. The online school offers the Switched on Schoolhouse curriculum by Alpha Omega, well known for many years. It offers flexible scheduling and customized curriculum plans. 804 N. 2nd Ave. East, Rock Rapids, IA 51246; 866-849-0131; www.americanacademyonlinedivision.com.

- *University of Missouri-Columbia* (grades 3–12 and college). U of M Columbia offers gifted courses, college prep—over two hundred courses in all. It also offers university-level courses and bachelor's degree completion programs. The lower-level courses are continuous enrollment. 800-609-3727; http://cdis.missouri.edu/go/nk6.asp.
- *Progress Academy K–12*. This online school is run by a homeschooling family with five children. They offer very flexible customer service and are creating a homeschooling community worldwide via their website. 866-516-2404; niqui@progressacademy.org; www.progressacademy.org.
- *e-Tutor K–12*. Since 1997, e-Tutor has been providing accredited and complete online instruction that takes the pressure off of parents by providing an imaginative curriculum created by teachers from all over the United States. Its program is web-based, so students can access it from anywhere that has an Internet connection, 24 × 7. www.e-tutor.com.
- *eTap Teaching Assistance Program* (K–12). eTap offer the core subjects and SAT, GED prep, and all state exit exams. It does not issue grades or diplomas, so parents should do their own grading and keep their records very well. Regarding diplomas, eTap suggests the GED for a nationally accredited diploma. Students at eTap work at their own pace, which is the number-one benefit cited by users. 2260 Park Ave., Laguna Beach, CA 92651; 949-497-2200; admin@etap.org; www.etap.org.
- *Time4Learning (T4L)* (K-8). This company offers a complete computer-based online program in math and language arts that is a popular core curriculum for many homeschooling families. Others like to use it as a supplement to their core subjects. Either way, T4L offers complete flexibility in its approach, providing different levels of instruction to a student who, for instance, is at one grade level in math and a different level in reading. 6400 N. Andrews Ave., Ste. 300, Fort Lauderdale, FL 33309; 954-771-0914; www.time4learning.com.
- *Regina Coeli Academy* (Catholic) (K–12). This is the first all-online Catholic homeschooling program. It is a liberal arts program with live interactive courses and self-paced, individual courses to provide the flexibility homeschoolers seek. www.reginacoeli.org.
- *Keystone High School*. This high school has been offering correspondence courses for over thirty years and an online course program for over ten years. It offers a complete curriculum or single courses, depending on the student's need. www.keystonehighschool.com.
- *Texas Tech Outreach Program*. This comprehensive program has courses for K–12, high school, college, and beyond college in both the credit and noncredit categories. Eligible high school students can take dual-credit courses or participate in academic enrichment programs on campus. All of the courses are written to the Texas Essential Knowledge and Skills (TEKS); the elementary, middle, and high

schools are accredited by the Texas Education Agency (TEA). Students can enroll in courses at any time and have up to six months to complete coursework. The Texas Tech distance learning courses are offered in a variety of formats, including online, print-based, video, and audio. Some courses require on-campus presence, so check first. www.depts.ttu.edu/oes.

- *Continental Academy* (high school completion only). This is an online high school that offers high school completion and a diploma to students at least sixteen years old who did not or could not complete a traditional high school program or those over eighteen who wish to complete their high school education. www.continentalacademy.com.

- *Branson Academy* (K–12). This online facility is a full-service school. It offers umbrella coverage in states that require it, and maintains complete records, both attendance and academic, and a high school diploma. Branson provides flexibility relative to your child's learning style and schedule so that she can study at her own pace. Its website provides extensive information about all of its services. Branson Academy, Inc., P.O. Box 326, Aromas, CA 95004; 831-726-3235; info@bransonacademy.net; http://bransonacademy.net.

- *Heritage Homeschool* (K–12). Heritage provides a complete Bible-based curriculum for K–12. It provides a high school diploma for those who successfully complete the program. The Heritage website also provides a valuable thumbnail statistical report on homeschooling success in standardized testing and other significant areas. 877-532-7665; infopack@heritagehomeschool.com; www.heritagehomeschool.com.

List 4.9. Tutors and Tutoring

Many of the Founding Fathers were homeschooled by their parents or were tutored by professional teachers who came to the home to provide instruction under the direction of the parents. Today, between online tutors and local bricks-and-mortar tutoring companies, homeschooling parents can turn to professional teachers for help regarding a variety of academic and artistic subjects. If you live in an urban area, one of these tutoring companies will be nearby; if not, you can access the wide variety of online tutors who provide excellent service and help.

- *Neufeld Learning Systems, Inc.* Individualized math tutoring and support. This company offers ten computer-assisted programs for grades K–10, ranging from numbers for K–3 to fractions, algebra, and geometry. 866-249-MATH; www.neufeld.com.
- *Ascend Tutoring* (online math). This very affordable tutoring service provides eighty-seven lessons per grade level, from grade 3 through the high school exit exam. To try a free demo, visit http://core-curriculum.com/CurricSol/index.html.
- *Dyslexia Tutoring & Testing.* Joy Moody, M.A., has a background in educational psychology. She provides materials, testing, and counseling for students with dyslexia and their parents. She provides parent training and a variety of materials to aid the dyslexic—and the nondyslexic too. 4594 E. Michigan Ave., Fresno, CA 93703; 559-251-9385; info@dyslexiatutoring.com; www.dyslexiatutoring.com.
- *Barton Reading & Spelling System* (dyslexia). Susan Barton developed this system of reading and spelling and has trained tutors to go on and work for themselves independently. See the Barton website for specific information for your locale. 2059 Camden Ave., Suite 186, San Jose, CA 95124; 408-559-3652; Info@BartonReading.com; www.bartonreading.com.

List 4.10. Homeschool Suppliers

These companies provide miscellaneous products to homeschoolers, from books to software and other supplies as well.

- *School-Tech.com* (multiple products). This website contains over six thousand products for all homeschool needs, from core subject textbooks to sports and recreation; videos and CD-ROMs, as well as books. Schoolmasters, 745 State Circle, Box 1941, Ann Arbor, MI 48106; www.school-tech.com.

- *Academic Superstore* (software). This is a massive discount product website, offering extensive software programs for large student discounts. Here you will find music programs, Adobe, Microsoft, and other lines of desirable products. 800-827-3440; www.tl. academicsuperstore.com.

- *Journey Ed.com* (software). Provider of deeply discounted student pricing for popular software programs and hardware. All of the name brands are available. 800-874-9001; www.journeyed.com.

- *Goodyear Books* (printed matter). Over two hundred resources for homeschooling families. From pre-K to grade 12, reading, writing, math, social studies, and science. P.O. Box 91858, Tucson, AZ 85752-1858; 888-511-1530; sales@goodyearbooks.com; www.goodyearbooks.com.

- *Academic Apparel* (graduation supplies). Offers quality graduation products for the homeschooler. Graduation robes, class rings, honor cords and stoles, all made to order. 800-626-5000; www.academicapparel.com or www.buyclassrings.com.

List 4.11. Testing and Test Prep

Standardized tests and evaluations for the lower grades are important to many homeschooling families who wish to have peace of mind that they are teaching their children properly. Of course the SAT, CEB, and ACT are important milestones in all college-bound students' lives, and homeschoolers are no different in this regard. Although many homeschooled students are entrepreneurs or attend college in a relaxed fashion, most still wish to attend college after completion of their high school work. There are a number of companies that supply standardized testing and assessment and others that offer college-entrance test prep. Here are some suggested ones.

Standardized Testing and Evaluation

- *Seton Home Testing.* This company provides affordable and fast CAT E tests for grades K–12. It provides the test materials, which are administered at home; it scores the test and returns the result to the parents, usually within two weeks. 800-542-1066 or 540-636-9990; www.setontesting.com.
- *Hewitt Homeschool Resources.* Hewitt has developed its own Personalized Achievement Summary System (PASS) standardized test specifically for homeschoolers in grades 3–8. Because many parents are sensitive to the stress and possible negative labeling connected with such tests, Hewitt has designed an evaluation that is not stressful or negative relative to the results. It is simply intended to allow parents to know if their methods are working as they wish them to. 800-890-4097; www.hewitthomeschooling.com.

SAT Test Prep

- *Powerscore.* This company offers affordable preparation for the LSAT, GMAT, GRE, and SAT tests, at numerous locations around the country and in weekend-only or weekday sessions. Their instructors all have scored in the 99th percentile of the SAT, and they are aware of homeschoolers' unique background of one-on-one teaching. 800-545-1750; www.powerscore.com.
- *Boston Test Prep.* BTP offers a 100-percent online SAT test prep at a reasonable price. Its staff comprises people from many walks of life, including online instructors. Its goals are to help students be ready to successfully take the test and to alleviate some of the stress. 99 High Street, 7th Floor, Boston, MA 02210; ph. 800-448-0671; fax 617-443-0991; www.bostontestprep.com.
- *Click and Climb – SAT math prep.* Provides very affordable online preparation in math. Tutors must have a bachelor's or master's degree plus four years of teaching experience. 800-671-1376; www.clickandclimb.com.

List 4.12. Homeschooling Resource Websites

The Internet has completely changed the face of homeschooling. It has reduced vast distances into global village proximity and enabled us to communicate with one another in the twinkling of an eye. These websites offer excellent information, resources, and sometimes even fun!

- *www.homeschoolnewslink.com* – The website of *The Link* homeschool publications. Includes resources, article, and product information to make your homeschooling experience easier and more successful.
- *www.homefires.com* – This site is maintained by Diane Flynn Keith, experienced homeschooling mom of two grown sons, popular conference speaker, and creator and author of *Carschooling*, published by Prima Publishing. Ms. Keith provides a daily subscription email feature called *Clickschooling*, which offers free resources to subscribers.
- *http://homeschooling.gomilpitas.com* – This website is filled with well-presented resources and information. It is part of a larger website that focuses on the Milpitas and Silicon Valley regions of California, but it has nationwide homeschooling information.
- *www.everythinghomeschooling.com* – This site features help on how to start homeschooling in your home and offers homeschooling products, lesson plans, lists of different associations, advice on child socialization, and much more.
- *www.midnightbeach.com/hs* – Also known as Jon's Midnight Beach, this is one of the oldest and broadest websites for homeschooling resources. It has much information relative to support groups and other important information.
- *www.homeschool.com* – Great site if you are new to homeschooling or need supplemental information.
- *www.home2teach.com* – Discussion board and links to support all homeschooling teaching needs.
- *www.homeschooling.about.com* – Superb website for beginners. Everything you need to get started.
- *www.homeschoolingonashoestring.com* – This site is targeted to frugally minded parents.
- *www.education.com* – Topics such as "multiple intelligences," pre-schooling, and "Ask the Teacher," in which teachers answer common questions regarding education.
- *www.homeschoollearning.com* – Site includes descriptions of the classical, Montessori, unschooling, and Reggio Emelia approaches.
- *www.montessori.edu* – This is perfect for the basics—history, philosophy, methods and materials used, plus locations of schools. It also

includes links that will help you in homeschooling your child using the method.

- *www.montessori.org* – Montessori's official home page is a great place to start if you're curious about the system itself.
- *www.unschooling.com* – Here beginners can find decent information in the "Library" section; those who have a bit more experience will find the message board and newsletter helpful.
- *www.unschooling.org* – Another great site for unschooling info. It serves as a resource and community center for like-minded parents.
- *www.homegrownfamilies.com* – A great Christian resource website that offers homeschooling supplies and support groups. Also offers apparel, newsletters, cooking recipes, and more.
- *www.laurelwoodbooks.com* – Offers homeschoolers a large variety of new and used books for any academic need.
- *www.homeschooldigitalid.com* – Provides home educators with personal ID cards, which will help save money on purchases for your homeschool needs.
- *www.nchea.org* – Excellent website for how to start homeschooling in Nebraska. Offers great resources and information regarding state laws and regulations.
- *www.home-educate.com* – Another very good site for those who seek to "break out of frames" of their children's education, Home Educate offers several interesting articles, resources, and a message board. Excellent for beginners.
- *www.borntoexplore.org* – A set of useful links for the homeschooling family, including Unschoolers Unlimited, a support network for parents who prefer to let their children learn their own way, at their own pace.

List 4.13. Websites for Miscellaneous Subjects and Information

These websites provide information about various topics and services that are very important and significant, but are not resources in the sense that the entries in the preceding list are, and do not fit in another list.

- *www.nheri.org: statistics, facts, and research* – This website is a must for those who want facts, statistics, and research information about homeschooling. The National Home Education Research Institute (NHERI) mission, as stated on the site, is to produce high-quality research on home education; to serve as a clearinghouse of research for home educators, researchers, policymakers, and the media; and to educate the public concerning the findings of all such research.

- *www.homeschoolmath.net* – Homeschool Math is a resource site for learning elementary math. Parents can create free worksheets and find teaching tips, free lesson plans, and links to games, quizzes, and interactive tutorials.

- *www.laurelwoodbooks.com* – This company has been serving homeschoolers for many years, with excellent used curriculum supplies and other materials. It has a sterling reputation for service and integrity. It even offers a unique book rental program.

- *www.homeschoolingadventures.com* – This is a friendly and helpful website for homeschooling resources. Beautifully and simply laid out, the site is basically a compilation of informative homeschooling links with an emphasis on work materials and tips to make your job easier. Covers a wealth of subjects from geography to math, as well as kindergarten to grade 12.

- *theswap.com* – This is a wonderful and venerable curriculum-swapping site featuring tons of resources. One of the best pages for finding used curricula, exchanging ideas, and getting general information on homeschooling. Highly recommended!

Part Five

Getting Your Homeschooled Student into College

List 5.1. College Admissions Considerations for Homeschoolers

One of the most-asked questions regarding homeschooling is "What about college?" The good news is that today, virtually every college and university in the country accepts homeschooled students. Some even seek homeschoolers because they tend to be serious about academic work. The following are some important things to keep in mind when helping your child plan for college.

- *Act early.* Decide early on, around ninth to tenth grade, which schools your child is interested in applying to and what their requirements are. The longer you wait, the lower your chances of being accepted.
- *Consider community colleges.* If you have one nearby, inquire into their acceptance of high school–age students taking college-level courses. Your child can begin taking college general education courses at age fifteen or sixteen and, after two years, transfer to a four-year school as a junior. This is much more economical than spending four years at a university. Community colleges have lower tuitions and housing is free, as your child will live at home.
- *Know the requirements for your target universities.* All universities have different requirements for the application process. Some simply plan their admissions by SAT or ACT scores, but the finest schools for actual learning take more into consideration—and some of the very finest do not even consider such entrance tests in their admissions profiles.
- *Have your child practice writing essays.* Universities that go beyond the standardized test scores have the student write an essay or two "on the spot" and then conduct some interviews with the student.
- *Help your child maintain a serious attitude about academics.* Homeschooled students do not make a habit of simply marking time in high school; they tend to view learning as serious business to be addressed and completed. Homeschoolers are not more intelligent than nonhomeschoolers, but they are generally *very* serious about their studies. This attitude in a college setting almost undoubtedly spells success.
- *Document your child's work beginning as early as possible.* Universities that go beyond the standardized test scores also often take into consideration the student's transcripts in assessing academic maturity—whether the transcripts are homemade or not. Therefore, tracking your child's work is very important.
- *Consider taking standardized tests.* Taking the SAT or the CEB and ACT might not be a bad idea, even if at the time they are not required. Your child may change her mind later on, and having these tests already taken can ease your mind about college admissions.

List 5.2. Homemade Transcripts and Portfolios for College

When you homeschool, you are not only the teacher but also the principal—the administrator. In addition to determining grades for your child's performance, you will have to create your child's transcripts and portfolios for college admissions, unless you are using a curriculum in a box or are enrolled in an independent study program (ISP) or online school for all of the grades. (See Appendix D for a sample transcript and portfolio.) Just as functioning as a teacher is not magical or mysterious, neither is functioning as the administrator. It simply takes regular attention to detail.

- *Learn to think in "educationalese."* This means that you train yourself to think the way school administrators do. Dance class counts as P.E. or performing arts. If your child takes voice lessons or piano, those qualify as fine arts electives or similarly labeled courses, depending on the colleges she is applying to. This becomes more important as your child reaches junior high or high school work.
- *Develop a system for equaling study hours with credit hours, just as schools do.* The Carnegie System (the standard used by many high schools) equates 120 hours with 1 credit unit. If your child studies English one hour per day, that is approximately 5 hours per week, 20 hours per month, so in a nine-month period that is 180 hours or 1.5 credits.
- *Keep all worksheets and other work done, all papers written, and the like.* If you have to submit a page of work, keep a copy on file. You will be glad if your portfolio contains more, rather than less, documentation.
- *Be judicious.* You don't have to include *everything* in your submission to a college. Your child's third-grade final math test isn't of importance to a dean of admissions!
- *Check what the ISP keeps track of.* Even if you use an ISP, it may not track credits for everything your child does, only what she does through the ISP. (Check on this when you enroll.) If your child takes a gymnastics or dance class independently and not through the ISP, she should get credit for it from you as either a P.E. credit or a performing arts credit, respectively.
- *Household duties can earn credits.* Grocery shopping, meal planning, and cooking can be credited as home economics. So can housecleaning and animal care. It is perfectly acceptable to grant credits for these activities, just as a public school would. Don't skimp on giving credit where it is due! Computer work—such as website design, web ad design, or computer-game design—can be rendered into transcript

form, including examples of the work done. Virtually any real interest and endeavor your child has can be described for credit; you simply have to think in the appropriate way.

- *Don't be afraid to give A grades.* If you keep all of the transcript records, don't be afraid to grant an A to your child for every course, if it is deserved. All grades are subjective, even in institutional schools, so you don't have to do much soul-searching to be truthful. You know whether your child actually knew the coursework in geometry or barely understood that a triangle has three angles. Straight-A students do exist—they earn such grades in schools every semester. Your child can be one, too, even though homeschooled.

- *Transcript or portfolio style?* Some colleges may prefer to see a portfolio format, which is more complete and detailed than a simple listing of courses and grades. Find out what your target schools want, as soon as possible.

- *Keep all documents in which your child is mentioned.* Keep all awards, certificates of achievement or completion, performance programs (especially those listing your child by name), honorable mentions in bulletins, articles written, or speeches given, for use someday in a transcript or portfolio.

- *Write yourself notes at the time of each event.* These will help you remember what the activity was. If there is an associated document, attach your notes to the item. If it is a performance program that does not actually name your child, note what he did in the program. You may be surprised what such a little detail can mean many years after the fact.

- *Store your documents safely.* A "red-rope" accordion file is great for each year—or maybe each half year, depending on how busy your child is. Or you can use one box for each year, just placing all of the paperwork into it as you go.

- *Work-study.* If your child does a part-time job or work of any kind, consider it as work-study; get a letter of recommendation or referral from the supervisor or person in charge, and also keep track of what your child does each day she works. Assisting a veterinarian is one example of such an activity. But helping out in a scrapbooking store, mowing lawns, or babysitting are all worthy of credit. You have to label it properly, that's all. Any volunteer work or community service your child engages in can be included in transcripts or portfolios. Some colleges want to know what type of *person*—not just the type of student—they are considering for admission.

- *Self-employed.* If you own your own business and your child helps out, don't forget to keep track of that, too. Working in a restaurant or retail store provides many different credit-worthy activities.
- *A final word.* All of these experiences can be significant to deans of admissions when applying for college—especially those colleges that do not make decisions based primarily on standardized test scores. A well-prepared homemade transcript can provide that little extra boost the admissions officer needs to see your child as a potential asset to the university.

List 5.3. Colleges That Seek Homeschoolers

In the past, many homeschoolers had a rough time getting through the admissions process because, among other things, they didn't have state-accredited diplomas or a class ranking. Recently, many colleges and universities have opened their doors to homeschoolers through traditional on-campus courses as well as distance-learning programs. With an estimated two million homeschoolers in the United States (per Dr. Brian Ray, citing National Home Education Research Institute statistics for 2002–2003; see www.nheri.org), news reports say some colleges are seeking them out because of their academic excellence. According to Chris Klicka, senior counsel and director of state and international relations for the Home School Legal Defense Association, "Several of the universities over the last few years have done surveys of their student body and have found the homeschool graduates in their student body have a higher grade-point average" (www.hslda.org). The following two lists provide some top choices among both traditional colleges and those that offer distance learning; note that some on the first list offer distance learning too.

Traditional Colleges

- *Concordia University, Irvine.* A four-year Christian liberal arts school based on Lutheran teachings, Concordia University, Irvine, is a school where many homeschoolers fit in and thrive. With a student/faculty ration of fifteen to one, Concordia offers fifty undergraduate majors and minors, nine graduate degrees, and an adult degree completion program. 1530 Concordia West, Irvine, CA 92612-3203; 949-854-8002; www.cui.edu.
- *Cottey College.* Located in a rural area of Missouri, Cottey College is a two-year independent, residential, liberal arts and sciences college for women with an enrollment of 350 students. In a diverse and supportive environment, women develop their potential for personal and professional lives of intellectual engagement and thoughtful action as leaders, learners, and citizens. The college seeks homeschoolers and maintains a high academic attitude that coincides with homeschool values. Cottey College, 1000 W. Austin, Nevada, MO 64712; 888-5-COTTEY (888-526-8839); www.cottey.edu.
- *St. Mary-of-the-Woods College.* This is a small women's college that actively seeks homeschooling girls. SMWC has high standards, and it wishes to attract students of intelligence and character who harmonize with those standards and hold themselves to high standards academically and personally. SMWC, Saint Mary-of-the-Woods, IN 47876-0067; 812-535-5151; smwc@smwc.edu; www.smwc.edu.

- *Vermont College: Union Institute and University.* VC offers undergraduate, graduate, and fine arts programs, awarding bachelor's degrees in liberal arts, master's degrees, and master of fine arts degrees. Life experience is recognized, and all programs are fully accredited. 36 College St., Montpelier, VT 05602; 800-336-6794.
- *Shimer College.* This small, independent, four-year liberal arts college uses the Great Books as its curriculum and has some classes with as few as twelve students, thus ensuring an excellent atmosphere for discussion, debate, and thought-provoking college work. Shimer seeks homeschoolers because they tend to fit right in with this supercharged, critical-thinking world. Shimer College, 3424 S. State St., Chicago, IL 60616; 312-235-3500; http://www.shimer.edu.
- *Patrick Henry College* (Christian). Patrick Henry College provides an approach that combines the classical liberal arts with practical, real-world experience. PHC was the first college to make a deliberate outreach to homeschool students. The distinctive qualities of PHC include practical apprenticeship methodology, a general education core based on the classical liberal arts, a dedication to mentoring Christian students, and a community life that promotes virtue, leadership, and strong, lifelong commitments to God, family, and society. PHC also offers distance learning courses. Patrick Henry College, One Patrick Henry Circle, Purcellville, VA 20132; 888-338-1776; admissions@phc.edu; www.phc.edu.

Distance Learning Colleges

- *Skidmore College.* Nestled in the middle of New York state's Hudson Valley, Skidmore, a small liberal arts college, is the oldest—and one of the foremost—among institutions of higher learning offering both on-campus as well as distance learning programs. Focusing on the merits of individual students, regardless of age or life circumstances, the University Without Walls at Skidmore College has developed as a perfect alternative for homeschoolers who don't want to be uprooted from their families, friends, and communities to obtain a college education. Skidmore College, 815 N. Broadway, Saratoga Springs, NY 12866.
- *Upper Iowa University.* Modeled after traditional correspondence learning programs, Upper Iowa University offers associate of arts degrees (liberal arts or general business concentration) or bachelor of science degrees in all standard fields. The Upper Iowa University External Degree program allows students to advance their education from their home. External Degree Office, P.O. Box 1861, Fayette, IA 52142; 888-877-3742; extdegree@uiu.edu; www.external.uiu.edu.

- *Trinity Western University FOCUS program.* Trinity Western University's FOCUS program offers an exciting way for college freshmen to engage in distance learning their first year and then either transfer their first-year credits to another university or attend TWU on campus the second year. The innovative TWU plan makes the initial transition from high school to college work a bit less stressful for the student, as it does not involve relocating. Trinity Western College also offers traditional campus college degree programs that welcome homeschool students. 7600 Glove Road, Langley, BC V2Y 1Y1; U.S. mailing address: P.O. Box 1409, Blaine, WA 98231-1409; 604-888-7511; www.focusyear.com.

- *Independent Study in Idaho.* ISI is a cooperative of four accredited Idaho institutions: Boise State University, Idaho State University, Lewis-Clark State College, and University of Idaho. The program delivers over one hundred college undergraduate, graduate, and high school distance education courses in online and print-based formats in over thirty subject areas. ISI college courses parallel their on-campus counterparts in content and completion standards. P.O. Box 443225, Moscow, ID 83844-3225; 208-885-6641 or 877-464-3246.

List 5.4. Distance Learning – Correspondence and Online Colleges and Universities

Online

The Internet has not only supported the growth of online K–12 programs; it has also made it possible for online university courses to flourish. Schools that formerly provided correspondence courses by regular mail have expanded their services to include their courses online, delivered via the Internet; other colleges have entered the distance learning world for the first time. Reliable figures put the number of online students (of all types and levels) at over 2.35 million and expanding rapidly. As with the bricks-and-mortar schools, each electronic university program has its own requirements for online attendance and admissions to the program, so check with each one first.

- *University of Colorado at Boulder – Independent Learning Program* (high school and college). *The Economist* ranked U of Colorado Boulder number eleven of all public universities in the world! Their online offerings are the same high quality, with the same credits, as those offered at the campus. This top-notch university offers an excellent value for the online student, by charging the in-state tuition—or even less in some instances. It offers a very popular concurrent enrollment program wherein a student with proper permission can receive completion credit for both high school and college. Contact the adviser for continuing education for testing requirements and related information. Division of Continuing Education & Professional Studies, 178 UCB, 1505 University Ave., Boulder, CO 80309-0178; in Denver, 303-492-5148; toll-free outside Denver, 800-331-2801; http://www.colorado.edu/cewww/contactus.htm.
- *The University of Tennessee Outreach and Continuing Education* (some online, some correspondence). Offers an independent study division for undergraduates, high school, and career enrichment certificates. It offers continuous enrollment (with up to nine months to complete), and university enrollment is not required. http://web.ce.utk.edu.
- *Colorado State University Distance Learning.* CSU has been offering its courses via distance learning techniques for over thirty-eight years, providing a broad spectrum of credit and noncredit, undergrad, graduate, and continuing education courses. Its distance learning classes are also delivered in the full variety of media—some are online, DVD/video, regular mail correspondence courses, or televised. If the student chooses to use the correspondence form of learning, the student must choose an exam proctor, complete a proctor agreement form, and file it with the university. http://www.learn.colostate.edu/distance.

- *The University of Kentucky.* UK offers a wide array of online courses in undergraduate, graduate, and doctoral levels. To use the online features, the student must be enrolled in the university and complete a tutorial in the use of the *Blackboard* software program, offered through the university's website. The UK Distance Learning program offers a number of uncommon courses—for instance, in animal work or veterinary medicine. There are a number of fees and costs, so the prospective student or parents should review the UK Distance Learning website carefully before making plans to enroll. http://www.uky.edu/DistanceLearning.

- *Brigham Young University Independent Study* (university and high school). The BYU IS division offers over six hundred university, high school, and personal enrichment courses, both online and traditional correspondence courses. The university program is accredited by the Northwest Commission on Colleges and Universities, and the independent study high school program is accredited by the Northwest Association of Accredited Schools (NAAS). http://ce.byu.edu/is/site.

- *Tompkins-Cortland Community College.* Tompkins-Cortland Community College (TC3) is located in Dryden, upstate New York; it is a college of SUNY, the State University of New York. Its flexible online program, CollegeNow, allows students to take one course at a time. In the CollegeNow section of the TC3 website, click on "Homeschooling" for complete admissions/registration and pricing details. http://www.sunytccc.edu/collegenow/homeschool/hs_student_course_schedule.asp.

Correspondence Only

- *Upper Iowa University* (full degree college). One of the few higher learning institutions to offer a full degree program via correspondence, UIU's program has been in existence since 1973 and has proved popular among homeschoolers as well as the general public. Of its seventeen degree offerings, only two require on-campus presence; the other fifteen are all correspondence courses! This unusual offering is a tremendous benefit to those who live far from the campus. External Degree Office, Upper Iowa University, P.O. Box 1861, Fayette, IA 52142; ph. 888-877-3742; fax 563-425-5353; extdegree@uiu.edu; www.external.uiu.edu (fast link to the External Degree page).

Appendix A: Homeschooling State by State

Despite the fact that it can be said that homeschooling is legal in all fifty states, the actual laws pertaining to homeschooling vary from state to state and range from no requirements at all to precise, strict laws regarding reporting, state intervention, and regular administering of standardized tests and reporting of their results.

The information offered here is not to be construed in any way as actual legal information. Only a lawyer can provide such information, and state laws can change greatly in a year's time. You are responsible for knowing the *current* laws in your state regarding homeschooling, and this is best learned from the statewide homeschooling association in the state itself. This is particularly true if you are relocating and need to know the laws of your new state. We have listed at least one such group for each state entry, except in the rare instance in which there is none.

With the advent of the "No Child Left Behind" laws, school officials are required to be more vigilant about truancy and attendance issues. As homeschoolers are often out and about in public during public school hours, homeschooling families need to be proactive in letting those around them know that they are not truants, but seriously pursuing the academic interests of their children. The information offered here is intended as an overview.

In states that provide more than one option for legal homeschooling, we provide the independent parent-teaching option. If the other options are equally attractive, we include them. If a section is not listed, that means that there is no requirement for that state as of the publication of this book. This includes the academic qualifications that parents must possess to teach their own children.

Alabama

In this state, in order to homeschool, parents must either start a church school or enroll in an existing one, or obtain a private tutor who is a certified teacher and monitored by the local school district.

Reporting: Parents must file a notice of intent with the local school district. Attendance records must be kept.

Compulsory Attendance: Ages seven to sixteen.

State Organization:
Christian Home Education Fellowship of Alabama (CHEF)
Box 20208, Montgomery, AL 36120
334-288-7229
www.chefofalabama.org
Convention: Sponsors annual convention; check the website for updates.

Alaska

This state provides a number of possible ways for parents to teach their own. Three of them are as follows: they can homeschool in the traditional fashion, enroll in a state-approved correspondence course, or register as a private school. Regular homeschooling has no requirements.

Compulsory Attendance: Ages seven to sixteen.

State Organization:
Alaska Private and Homes Educators Association (APHEA)
P.O. Box 141764, Anchorage, AK 99514
907-376-9382
Any board member: board@aphea.org
www.aphea.org
Convention: Sponsors an annual convention; check the website for updates.

Arizona

Reporting: The parents must file an affidavit of intent to homeschool within thirty days of beginning to, along with a certified copy of the child's birth certificate.

Compulsory Attendance: Ages six to sixteen. Homeschoolers can wait until age eight, with a written request.

Required Subjects: Math, reading, grammar, science, and social studies.

State Organization:

Arizona Families for Home Education (AFHE) (Christian)

P.O. Box 2035, Chandler, AZ 85244-2035

602-235-2673

www.afhe.org

AFHE advises that the email form on its website is the best way to contact it.

Convention: Annual convention; check the website for updates.

Arkansas

Reporting: Written notice of intent to homeschool must be filed annually with the local superintendent of schools by August 15 for the fall semester, by December 15 for the spring, or fourteen days before removing the child from public school. (The Notice of Intent and Waiver are both available for download at the Education Alliance website that follows.)

Compulsory Attendance: Ages five to seventeen (a waiver can be obtained from the state for children under age six on September 15).

Testing: The child must take the same standardized tests as public school students in grades 3 through 9.

State Organization:

The Education Alliance

414 S. Pulaski Suite 9, Little Rock, AR 72201

ph. 501-978-5503; fax 501-375-7040

info@arkansashomeschool.org

www.arkansashomeschool.org

Conventions: Sponsors an annual convention; check the website for updates. There is also a Northwest Arkansas Home School Convention; check the Education Alliance website for information.

California

This state provides for parents to qualify as a private homeschool, hiring a private tutor, or enrolling in either a private ISP or a public school ISP. In the public school ISP, the school does everything a regular public school would in terms of record-keeping, attendance requirements, and so on.

Reporting: To qualify as a private school, parents must file an affidavit of intent with the state superintendent of schools each year between October 1 and 15. Attendance records must be kept.

Compulsory Attendance: Ages six to eighteen.

Required Subjects: The same as those in the public school in the English language. Parents must inquire independently as to what the syllabus is for each year.

State Organizations:

1. HomeSchool Association of California (HSC) (secular)

P.O. Box 77873, Corona, CA 92877

The website, www.hsc.org, contains numerous email addresses that address specific issues or questions.

Convention: Sponsors annual Home = Education Conference; check the website.

2. Christian Home Educators Association of California (CHEA)

12440 E. Firestone Blvd., Ste. 311, Norwalk, CA 90650

562-864-2432

info@cheaofca.org

www.cheaofca.org

Convention: Sponsors annual convention; check the website.

Colorado

Here parents can be designated as a homeschool, enroll in a private school that allows parents to teach at home, or hire a tutor.

Reporting: Parents must file an annual notice of intent to homeschool with the local superintendent fourteen days before they begin teaching. They must also maintain attendance records, standardized test results, and immunization records.

Compulsory Attendance: Ages seven to sixteen. For homeschools, it is 172 days per year, four hours per day.

Required Subjects: Math, reading, writing, literature, public speech, science, civics, history and the Constitution of the United States.

Testing: Parents are responsible to administer standardized tests for grades 3, 5, 7, 9, and 11 or have their child evaluated by a person they deem qualified.

State Organizations:

This state does not have a statewide organization. However, the following will provide state information:

Colorado Academy of Independent Learners (CAIL)

21135 Warriors Path Dr., Peyton, CO 80831

Contact: Kerry Kantor, ph./fax 719-749-0200

info@cail-school.org

www.cail-school.org

"CAIL offers families the opportunity to be part of a private school, with many of the advantages a private school can offer while at the same time deriving all the benefits of a home-based education program."

Connecticut

Reporting: Parents can file a notice of intent within ten days of beginning to teach. A portfolio showing completed work is required to be kept.

Compulsory Attendance: Ages five to eighteen, but parents can file a waiver for five- or six-year-olds at their school district; 180 days per year.

Required Subjects: Math, English, spelling, grammar, writing, reading, geography, U.S. history and citizenship, government—local, state, and national.

State Organizations:
1. CT Homeschool Network (CHN) (secular)
P.O. Box 115, Goshen, CT 06756
www.cthomeschoolnetwork.org
Convention: Sponsors an annual conference; check the website for updates.

2. The Education Association of Christian Homeschoolers (TEACH)
10 Moosehorn Rd., West Granby, CT 06090
860-435-2890
teachct@snet.net
www.teachct.org
Convention: Sponsors an annual conference; check the website for updates.

Delaware

This state provides a rather unique twist in that, besides the regular one-family homeschool or the one-family public school ISP, it also provides for a multi-family homeschool, in which not all of the children are related as brothers or sisters. We provide information for the one-family choices.

Reporting: Parents must report attendance to the Department of Education on or before July 31 each year. They must also provide an annual statement of enrollment on the last day of public school attendance in September, on state-approved forms.

Compulsory Attendance: Ages five to sixteen, but parents can delay start until child is older with written permission from the school district; 180 days per year for all choices.

State Organizations:
1. Delaware Home Education Association
info@dheaonline.org
www.dheaonline.org

2. Tri-State Homeschool Network (DE/MD/PA) Christian
P.O. Box 7193, Newark, DE 19714-7193
302-456-3545
tristatepres@msn.com
Convention: None.

District of Columbia

Reporting: No notice is required unless the child has already been enrolled in public school. Attendance records are required to be kept.

Compulsory Attendance: Ages five to eighteen, during the same time as the public schools.

State Organization:

Christian Home Educators of DC
5231 Kansas Ave. NW, Washington, DC 20011
ph. 202-829-5041; fax 202-526-4108
slanda19@aol.com
Convention: None.

Florida

This state provides that parents can homeschool independently or as a qualified homeschool co-op sort of entity, which is a private school corporation of homeschooling families. At present, the only difference between the two choices is that the qualifying process eliminates the need for annual standardized testing, to which independent families are subject. The following are for these families.

Reporting: Parents must file a notice of intent to homeschool with the local school district within thirty days of beginning to officially teach. They also have to maintain a portfolio of the child's work and a record of the materials used.

Compulsory Attendance: Ages six to sixteen; 180 days are required in the public schools, but there is currently no specific requirement for homeschoolers.

Testing: An annual standardized test has to be administered by a certified teacher, or the child can simply be evaluated by a certified teacher.

State Organizations:

Florida Parent-Educators Association (FPEA)
7682 Municipal Dr., Orlando, FL 32819
ph. 877-ASK–FPEA (877-275-3732)
fax 407-363-9241
www.fpea.com

Conventions: Each of the following has an annual fair; check the websites for updates.

1. Coastal Florida Curriculum Fair
Central Assembly of God, 6767 20th St., Vero Beach, Florida 32966
www.coastalfair.com

2. North Central Florida Homeschool Fair, Gainesville
www.ncfhomeschoolfair.com

3. Freedom Academy of Learning Convention
www.freedomacademyoflearning.org

Georgia

In this state, parents must have a high school diploma or its equivalent (GED) to teach their children.

Reporting: Parents must file a notice of intent with the local school district within thirty days of beginning teaching the first year and by September 1 each year after that. Monthly attendance records must be filed with the school district and an annual progress report at the end of each school year.

Compulsory Attendance: Ages six to sixteen; 180 days per year, four-and-a-half hours per day.

Required Subjects: Math, reading, language arts (typically spelling, grammar, composition), science, and social studies.

Testing: The parents must administer a standardized test at the end of grades 3, 6, 9, and 12 and must keep the results on file for potential review by the school district.

State Organization:
Georgia Home Education Association (GHEA) (Christian)
258 Sandy Lake Circle, Fayetteville GA 30205
ph. 770-461-3657; fax 501-638-5264
info@ghea.org
www.ghea.org
Convention: GHEA sponsors an annual conference; check the website for updates.

Hawaii

Reporting: Parents must file a notice of intent to homeschool with the local school district before beginning to teach and notice of conclusion within five days of having ended the school year. They must also maintain a record of the curriculum materials used.

Compulsory Attendance: Ages six to eighteen.

Required Subjects: This area is not strictly defined—which will suit most homeschoolers to a T. It requires the parents to teach the child educational as well as up-to-date and useful skills, taking into account the child's natural skills and interests.

Testing: The parents must administer a standardized test of their choice in grades 3, 5, 8, and 10 and file it in an annual evaluation/progress report with the local school officials.

State Organizations:

1. Christian Homeschoolers of Hawaii (CHOH)
c/o 921739 Makakilo Dr. #18, Kapolei, HI 96707
808-689-6398
www.christianhomeschoolersofhawaii.org
This group has a network of local support groups around the islands; check for your local contact.

2. Catholic Homeschoolers of Hawaii
esther@catholicweb.com
www.catholichomeschoolhawaii.com

3. Hawaii Homeschool Association
P.O. Box 893513, Mililani, HI 96789
info@hawaiihomeschoolassociation.org
Convention: CHOH sponsors an annual conference; check the website for updates.

Idaho

This state is very lenient in its current homeschool laws and atmosphere. Parent are required to provide the child with an education.

Compulsory Attendance: Ages seven to sixteen, for the same number of days as the public schools.

State Organization:

Christian Homeschoolers of Idaho State (CHOIS)
PO. Box 45062, Boise, ID 83711-5062
info@chois.org
www.chois.org/convention.html
Convention: CHOIS sponsors an annual convention; check the website for updates.

Illinois

A very lenient state. The former state director of the Department of Education was quite openly supportive of homeschooling in the late 1990s.

The atmosphere still seems very friendly here, but check for yourself and assume nothing.

Compulsory Attendance: Ages seven to seventeen; not specifically defined for homeschoolers, but approximately 176 days for public schools.

Required Subjects: Math, reading, writing, spelling, grammar, comprehension, composition, physical sciences, biology, social sciences, fine art, health, and physical education.

State Organizations:

1. Christian Home Educators Coalition
P.O. Box 34885, Chicago, IL 60634-0322
ph. and fax 773-278-0673

2. Illinois Christian Home Educators (ICHE)
P.O. Box 307, Russell, IL 60075-0307
847-603-1259
info@iche.org

3. Home Oriented Unique Schooling Experience (H.O.U.S.E.) (nonreligious)
847-622-5200
info@illinoishouse.org
Convention: Both H.O.U.S.E. and ICHE sponsor an annual conference; check the websites for updates.

Indiana

Currently there is a progressive homeschooling atmosphere here.

Reporting: The state has no requirement, but allows for a discretionary option for the state superintendent of education to request a notice be given. Attendance records must be maintained and made available if requested by local officials.

Compulsory Attendance: Ages seven to eighteen; approximately 180 days per year.

State Organizations:

1. Indiana Association of Home Educators (IAHE) (Christian)
320 East Main St., Greenfield, IN 46140
317-467-6244
iahe@inhomeeducators.org
www.inhomeducators.org

2. Indiana Foundation for Home Schooling
P.O. Box 17385, Indianapolis, IN 46217
317-308-6411 or 800-465-2505

info@IndianaHomeSchooling.org

Convention: AHE sponsors an annual conference; check the website for updates.

Iowa

In this state, parents may teach their own without having to hold a diploma or degree; they may choose to work under the oversight of a state-licensed teacher. There is virtually no difference between the two, unless the parent feels unqualified, of course.

Reporting: Parents must file an annual form called the "Competent Private Instruction Report Form" in duplicate with the local school district before the first day of public school or within fourteen days of the child's removal from public school.

Compulsory Attendance: Ages six to sixteen; 148 days per year.

Testing: Parents have until May 1 each year to complete a standardized test and then file the results with the local school officials by June 30, along with a portfolio of the child's work.

State Organizations:

1. Network of Iowa Christian Home Educators (NICHE)
Box 158, Dexter, Iowa 50070
515-830-1614 or 800-723-0438 (in Iowa)
niche@netins.net
www.the-niche.org

2. Iowans Dedicated to Educational Alternatives (IDEA) (unschooling)
kdiltz@avalon.net
www.avalon.net/~pdiltz/idea
Convention: None

Kansas

In this state, parents can operate their homeschool as a nonaccredited private school or become affiliated with an accredited private school and be an extension "campus," or for high schoolers, there is a religious exemption available. Check with the state Department of Education. The teaching parents must also be competent, but at the local level there is no definition of what constitutes competence.

Reporting: The parents must register the name and address of their private school with the state board of education.

Compulsory Attendance: Ages seven to eighteen; 186 days or 1,116 hours per year.

State Organization:

Christian Home Educators Confederation Of Kansas
P.O. Box 1332, Topeka, KS 66601
785-272-6655
www.kansashomeschool.org
Convention: None

Kentucky

Parents should know what is expected of them in advance in this state, as the atmosphere is not quite as lenient as in some other states. That is not to say that it is dictatorial, rather that homeschooling is not as flexible as in states that have no reporting or testing requirements. Remember that when dealing with any governmental agency, ignorance of the law is no defense.

Reporting: Parents must notify the local school district of their intent to homeschool and the children's names, within two weeks of the beginning of the school year. An attendance record must be kept.

Compulsory Attendance: Ages six to sixteen; 185 days per year

Required Subjects: Math, reading, spelling, grammar, writing, history, and civics.

State Organizations:

1. Bluegrass Home Educators
600 Shake Rag Rd., Waynesburg KY 40489-8371
http://kyhomeschool.info

2. Christian Home Educators of Kentucky (CHEK)
691 Howardstown Rd., Hodgenville, KY 42748; 270-358-9270
www.chek.org
Convention: Sponsors an annual conference; check the website for updates.

3. Kentucky Home Education Association (KHEA)
P.O. Box 51591, Bowling Green, KY 42102-5891
270-779-6574
mail@khea.info
Convention: Sponsors the KY Homeschool Conference & Book Fair; check
   the website for updates.

Louisiana

Here, parents can operate as a homeschool private school or a board-of-education-approved homeschool. There is virtually no difference between them.

The private school has no record-keeping requirements or testing requirements. For parents not operating as a private school, the following rules apply:

Reporting: An annual application and copy of the child's birth certificate must be filed with the local board of education within fifteen days after the family begins homeschooling.

Compulsory Attendance: Ages seven to eighteen; 180 days per year.

Required Subjects: Comparable to that taught in the public schools, and must include a study of the Federalist Papers and the Declaration of Independence.

Testing: With the renewal application, the parents must submit evidence that their program is at least comparable to the public school offering. The only record-keeping requirement is whatever is necessary to satisfy this evidence requirement.

State Organization:

1. Christian Home Educators Fellowship (CHEF) of Louisiana
P.O. Box 226, Maurice, LA 70555
888-876-CHEF (888-876-2433)
www.chefofla.org

2. Louisiana Home Education Network (LAHEN) (nonreligious)
PMB 700, 602 W. Prien Lake Rd., Lake Charles, LA 70601
Conventions: Possibly none; check the websites for updates.

Maine

Parents can teach their children at home.

Reporting: Parents must file an annual notice of intent to homeschool within ten days of the beginning of the school year. A copy of the notice must be provided to the local school district and the commissioner of education. Copies of all material filed with the school district must be kept until the child has completed his or her homeschooling.

Compulsory Attendance: Ages seven to seventeen; 175 days per year.

Required Subjects: Math, language arts, English, social studies, physical education, science, health, fine arts, and state studies, between grades 6 and 12, and computer skills between grades 7 and 12.

Testing: Each year the parents must administer either a standardized test or a local school district test, or have the child's progress reviewed by a certified teacher.

State Organizations:

1. Homeschoolers of Maine (HOME) (Christian)
P.O. Box 159, Camden, ME 04843-0159
207-763-2880
www.homeschoolersofmaine.org
Convention: Sponsors annual convention; check the website for updates.

2. Maine Home Education Association (nonreligious)
350 Duck Pond Rd., Westbrook, ME 04092
mainehomeed@yahoo.com
www.geocities.com/mainehomeed

Maryland

Here parents can either simply teach their children at home or provide home instruction under the supervision of a school or church that is recognized by the state. The requirements are somewhat vague, so the homeschooling parents should investigate closely.

Reporting: Parents must file a notice of intent at least fifteen days before beginning to teach the first year. Each year after that, they must inform the local school district if they will be homeschooling for that year. Parents must keep a portfolio of the student's work and materials that have been taught, and be able to provide them at least three times per school year.

Compulsory Attendance: None specified per se.

Required Subjects: Same as the public schools are required to provide: math, English, social studies, science, music, art, physical education, and health.

Testing: None.

State Organizations:
1. Christian Home Educators Network (CHEN)
P.O. Box 2010, Ellicott City, MD 21043
chenmemb@chenmd.org
www.chenmd.org

2. Maryland Home Education Association (MHEA) (nonreligious)
9085 Flamepool Way, Columbia, MD 21045
ph. 410-730-0073; fax 410-964-5720
MSmith@mhea.com
www.mhea.com

Convention: MHEA sponsors an annual conference; check the website for updates.

Massachusetts

This state requires the parents to obtain advance approval by local school authorities. What this entails seems to have varied in recent years, so find out your local school district's current requirements as soon as you decide to homeschool here.

Reporting: Beyond the approval process, there is currently no reporting requirement. However, since the atmosphere in this state has been very draconian in years past, it might be wise to keep records of attendance, track the child's work and progress, and so on anyway. When it comes time to apply to colleges, this information will come in handy for developing transcripts and showing completion of certain work.

Compulsory Attendance: Ages six to sixteen, with 900 hours per year for elementary students, 990 hours for secondary school students.

Required Subjects: Arithmetic, reading, writing, English language skills including grammar, art, music, geography, the U.S. Constitution and history, citizenship, physical education.

Testing: There is no specified requirement, but at the time approval is sought, the approving authority may require standardized testing as a condition of approval. Thus it is important to inquire in detail first, *before* you make a hard and fast decision about homeschooling here.

State Organizations:

1. Massachusetts Home Learning Association (nonreligious)
P.O. Box 536, Swampscott, MA 01907
mhla@mhla.org
http://mhla.org

2. Massachusetts Homeschool Organization of Parent Educators (MASSHOPE) (Christian)
46 South Rd, Holden, MA 01520
508-829-0973
www.masshope.org
Convention: Sponsors annual conference; check the website for updates.

3. Advocates for Home Education in Massachusetts (AHEM) (nonreligious)
P.O. Box 1307, Arlington, MA 02474
info@AHEM.info
www.ahem.info
Convention: Learning in Our Own Way (www.learninginourownway.com). Produced by esteemed unschooling expert Patrick Farenga; check the website for updates.

Michigan

The homeschooling laws in this state have a number of twists and turns that prospective homeschooling parents need to address. As always, seek the advice of the statewide organizations before doing anything.

Compulsory Attendance: Ages six to sixteen. Must conform to the local public school.

Required Subjects: Math, English grammar, reading, literature, spelling, writing, history, civics, science, history and civics (see statute for specifics).

State Organizations:

1. Homeschooling Michigan
P.O. Box 813, Clarkston, MI 48347-0813
www.homeschoolingmichigan.com

2. Information Network for Christian Homes (INCH)
4934 Cannonsburg Rd., Belmont, MI 49306-9614
616-874-5656
www.inch.org
Convention: Sponsors an annual conference; check the website for updates.

Minnesota

Reporting: Parents must file a form called a "Non-Public Education Compulsory Instructions Report" with the local school superintendent by October 1 of each school year. Thereafter they have to submit a quarterly report to the superintendent showing the child's progress.

Compulsory Attendance: Ages seven to sixteen; no attendance requirement.

Required Subjects: Math, reading, writing, fine arts, literature, history, government, geography, science, health and physical education.

Testing: An annual standardized test, approved in advance by the superintendent must be administered.

State Organizations:

Minnesota Association of Christian Home Educators (MACHE)
P.O. Box 32308, Fridley, MN 55432
763-717-9070 or 866-717-9070
info@mache.org
www.mache.org
Convention: Sponsors an annual convention; check the website for updates.

Minnesota Homeschoolers Alliance (MHA)
P.O. Box 40486, St. Paul, MN 55104
612-288-9662 (Twin City Metro Area)
888-346-7622 (outside Twin Cities)
www.homeschoolers.org
Convention: Sponsors an annual convention; check the website for updates.

Mississippi

This is currently a lenient state in terms of its statutory requirements.

Reporting: Parents must file a notice of intent by September 15 of each year with the local school district's office.

Compulsory Attendance: Ages six to seventeen. No annual attendance requirement.

State Organization:

Mississippi Home Education Association (MHEA) (Christian)
mhea@mhea.net
www.mhea.net
Convention: Sponsors an annual conference; check the website for updates.

Missouri

Reporting: The parents must keep attendance records of the hours taught, the subjects taught, the social activities the child engages in, and examples of the child's academic work.

Compulsory Attendance: Ages seven to sixteen; 1,000 hours per year; 600 in the required subjects, 400 of those at the homeschool location.

Required Subjects: Math, language arts, reading, social studies, and science.

State Organizations:

1. Families for Home Education (FHE) (secular)
P.O. Box 742, Grandview, MO 64030
816-767-9825
1983@fhe-mo.org
www.fhe-mo.org

2. Missouri Association of Teaching Christian Homes, Inc. (MATCH)
2203 Rhonda Dr., West Plains, MO 65775
information@match-inc.org
www.match-inc.org
Convention: None.

Montana

Reporting: Parents must file an annual notice of intent to homeschool with the local school superintendent. Must maintain attendance and immunization records, available for review by the local school superintendent upon request.

Compulsory Attendance: Ages seven to sixteen or completion of eighth grade; 720 hours per year, grades 1–3; 1,080 hours per year for grades 4–12.

Required Subjects: The same as the public schools teach.

State Organization:

Montana Coalition of Home Educators (MCHE) (secular)
white@imt.net
www.mtche.org

Convention: Sponsors an annual convention; check the website for updates.

North Carolina

Parents must possess a high school diploma or GED to homeschool.

Reporting: File a notice of intent with the local school district before beginning.

Compulsory Attendance: Ages seven to sixteen; at least nine months per year.

Required Subjects: None specifically, but the annual standardized test must cover math, reading, English grammar, and spelling.

Testing: Annual test as just noted.

State Organizations:

1. North Carolina African-American Homeschoolers (all-inclusive)
ncaahomeschoolers@yahoo.com
http://ncaahomeschoolers.tripod.com

2. Homeschool Alliance of North Carolina
ha-nc@ha-nc.org
www.ha-nc.org

3. North Carolinians for Home Education (NCHE)
4326 Bland Road, Raleigh, NC 27609
ph. 919-790-1100; fax 919-790-1892
nche@nche.com
www.nche.com
Convention: NCHE sponsors an annual conference; check the website for updates.

Nebraska

Here homeschooling is considered in the same category as a private school.

Reporting: Parents must file a notice of intent with the state commissioner of education by August 1 or thirty days before starting to teach.

Compulsory Attendance: Ages six to eighteen; 1,032 hours per year for elementary grades, which is equivalent to 180 days at 5.75 hours per day, and 1,080 hours per year for high school grades—180 days at six hours per day.

Required Subjects: Math, language arts (reading, grammar, spelling, and so on), science, health, and social studies.

State Organization:

Nebraska Christian Home Educators Association (NCHEA) (statement of faith required)

P.O. Box 57041, Lincoln, NE 68505-7041
nchea@alltel.net
www.nchea.org
Convention: Sponsors an annual conference; check the website for updates.

Nevada

Parents in this state have to prove their qualification to teach their children by demonstrating that they (1) have one year of homeschooling experience in the United States, or (2) possess a teaching credential from any state, or (3) possess a signed statement that the parent has read and understood the Nevada statutes on homeschooling. These and other requirements here are very nebulous—a source of potential trouble.

Reporting: Parents have to file an annual written report that sets forth evidence that the child is receiving the level of education approved by the state board of education.

Compulsory Attendance: Ages seven to seventeen; 180 days or the equivalent.

Required Subjects: Math, English, science, social studies. As practical, the fine arts, health, physical education, and computer instruction.

State Organization:
Nevada Homeschool Network (NHN)
P.O. Box 1212, Carson City, NV 89702
888-842-2606
briansmom99@yahoo.com
www.nevadahomeschoolnetwork.com
Convention: Sponsors an annual conference; check the website for updates.

New Hampshire

In the early 1990s, this state was very strict in its homeschooling laws and enforcement. Be sure to check whether this is still the case.

Reporting: Parents must file a notice of intent within thirty days of withdrawing a child from public school or having moved into the district, with the local school district, a private school principal, or the state education commissioner. A portfolio must be maintained containing a list of reading materials used, samples of the child's writing, workbooks, and other materials used.

Compulsory Attendance: Ages six to sixteen; no daily attendance requirement.

Required Subjects: Math, reading, spelling, writing, language, health, history, art, music appreciation, government, and U.S. and New Hampshire constitutional history.

Testing: By July 1 each year, the parents must file the results from a standardized test, the results of an assessment test used by the local school district, a written evaluation of the student by a certified teacher, or some other standard of evaluation as indicated by the local school board.

State Organizations:

1. New Hampshire Homeschool Coalition (NHHC)
P.O. Box 2224, Concord, NH 03302
603-437-3547
webmaster@nhhomeschooling.org
www.nhhomeschooling.org

2. Christian Home Educators of New Hampshire (CheNH) (requires a statement of faith)
P.O. Box 961, Manchester, NH 03105
www.chenh.org
Convention: Sponsors an annual conference; see the website for updates.

New Jersey

This is a very liberal state regarding governmental jurisdiction over homeschooling.

Compulsory Attendance: Ages six to sixteen; no daily attendance specified, but 180 days is required of the public schools.

Required Subjects: Code specifies that instruction must be equivalent to that offered in the public schools.

State Organizations:

1. New Jersey Homeschooling Association (NJHA)
P.O. Box 1386, Medford, NJ 08055
609-953-0468
jerseyhome@yahoo.com
www.geocities.com/jerseyhome

2. Education Network of Christian Homeschoolers of New Jersey (ENOCH)
Box 308, Atlantic Highlands, NJ 07716
732-291-7800
www.enochnj.org

3. Catholic Homeschoolers of New Jersey (CHNJ)
info@chnj.org
http://chnj.brinkster.net/index2.htm
Conventions: #2 and #3 sponsor annual conferences; check their websites for updates.

New Mexico

Parents must possess a high school diploma or its equivalent.

Reporting: Parents must file a notice of intent within thirty days of beginning to homeschool and by April 1 of each year thereafter.

Compulsory Attendance: Ages five to eighteen or high school graduation, whichever occurs first. Same number of days as the local public schools.

Required Subjects: Math, reading, language arts, science, and social studies.

State Organization:

Christian Association of Parent Educators (CAPE-NM)

www.cape-nm.org

Convention: Sponsors annual conference; check the website for updates.

New York

This state is one of the most stringent in terms of record-keeping and reporting requirements that parents must submit to.

Reporting: Attendance records must be maintained and, if necessary, shown to the local superintendent of education. Quarterly reports must be filed with the superintendent, demonstrating the hours of instruction in that quarter, a description of what has been covered in each subject, and a letter grade or evaluation in each subject.

Compulsory Attendance: Ages six to sixteen or high school graduation.

Required Subjects: K–12: Math, spelling, reading, writing, English, U.S. history, geography, health, science, fire safety, substance abuse, patriotism, citizenship, and traffic safety. In grades 7 and 8, physical education and library skills are added. In grades 9 through 12, social studies, government, and economics are added.

Testing: Parents must file an annual assessment with the local superintendent of education by June 30. This comes from standardized test results every other year between grades 4 and 8 and every year for grades 9 through 12. The student must score above the 33rd percentile or risk having the homeschool be placed on probation. In the alternate years of the testing, the assessment can be prepared by a third party approved of by the superintendent.

State Organizations:

1. APPLE Family & Homeschool Group

P.O. Box 2036, No. Babylon, NY 11703

info@APPLEnetwork.US

www.applenetwork.us/ny/apple.html

2. New York State Loving Education at Home (LEAH) (Christian)

www.nysleah.org

3. Parents Instructing Challenged Children (PICC)
Barb Mulvey, 700 W. Liberty St., Rome, NY 13440-3942
ph. 315-339-5524 after 2:00 P.M. on weekdays
picc@twcny.rr.com
www.piccnys.com
Conventions: #2 sponsors two annual conventions; check the website for
   updates.

North Dakota

This state is the most stringent in terms of the requirements necessary for parents to teach their own children. As noted later, Pennsylvania requires parents to possess a high school diploma or the equivalent. North Dakota requires parents who do not possess a teaching certificate or B.A., but do possess a high school diploma or equivalent, to be monitored by a certified teacher during the first two years of homeschooling. After that, if the child scores below the 50th percentile on standardized tests, monitoring of the parents must continue. Note: If you have a child who is developmentally disabled, there are more strict requirements for reporting and the like, so look carefully into these before beginning to homeschool.

Reporting: Each year a notice of intent to homeschool must be filed with the local superintendent fourteen days before the beginning of homeschooling or, in the case of new arrivals to the school district, on the fourteenth day of residency. The parents must also maintain an annual record of the subjects completed and the child's progress through them, by assessments and standardized test results.

Compulsory Attendance: Ages seven to sixteen; 175 days per year, but only four hours per day or seven hundred hours per year.

Required Subjects: Math, English language skills—reading, composition, grammar, spelling, creative writing; social studies, U.S. history, U.S. Constitution, government, science, geography, physical education, and health.

Testing: Standardized tests are required to be administered in grades 4, 6, 8, and 10. The test must be administered by a certified teacher and the results submitted to the local school superintendent. If the child scores below the 30th percentile, a professional determination regarding learning disability must be obtained and the parents must submit a remedial plan to the superintendent.

State Organization:

North Dakota Home School Association (NDHSA) (Christian; statement
   of faith required)
P.O. Box 7400, Bismarck, ND 58507
office@ndhsa.org

www.ndhsa.org

Convention: Sponsors an annual conference; check the website for updates.

Ohio

Parents must have a high school diploma or equivalent. Otherwise, they must work under the direction of a certified teacher.

Reporting: An annual notice of intent must be submitted to the local superintendent. No other records are required.

Compulsory Attendance: Ages six to eighteen; 900 hours per year.

Required Subjects: Math, language arts, U.S. and state history, geography, physical education, health, arts, science, and first aid.

Testing: Each year's notice of intent must be accompanied by either standardized test scores, a written report demonstrating the student's satisfactory progress, or some other assessment approved by the local superintendent.

State Organization:
Christian Home Educators of Ohio (CHEO)
117 W. Main Street, Ste. #103, Lancaster, OH 43130
ph. 740-654-3331; fax 740-654-3337
Cheo@cheohome.org
www.cheohome.org

Conventions: CHEO sponsors an annual convention; see the website for updates. There is also an annual Cincinnati Homeschool Convention; check www.cincinnatihomeschoolconvention.com for updates.

Oklahoma

This state distinguished itself a few years ago by including parents' rights to teach their own children at home as "an other means" of education as part of its constitution.

Compulsory Attendance: Ages five to eighteen; 180 days per year.

Required Subjects: Math, reading, writing, science, health, safety, physical education, citizenship, conservation, and U.S. Constitution.

State Organizations:
1. Home Educators' Resource Organization (HERO) (secular)
http://oklahomahomeschooling.org

2. Oklahoma Christian Home Educators' Consociation (OCHEC)
3801 NW 63rd St., Bldg. 3, Ste. 236, Oklahoma City, OK 73116
405-810-0386
staff@ochec.com

www.ochec.com

Convention: #2 sponsors an annual convention; check the website for updates.

Oregon

This state is very lenient in its requirements. There are no reporting requirements except to notify the local school district in writing when the child begins to be homeschooled and if the family relocates, notifying the new district again. There are no annual attendance laws or required subjects specified.

Compulsory Attendance: Ages seven to eighteen or completion of twelfth grade.

Testing: A state-approved assessment test must be administered in grades 3, 5, 8, and 10, administered by a qualified third party. If the child has been removed from public school, the first such test must be administered within eighteen months of that removal. Families with children with disabilities have further requirements, so check first if this is your case.

State Organizations:
1. Oregon Home Education Network (OHEN)
P.O. Box 1386, Beaverton, OR 97075
Message line: 503-321-5166
info@ohen.org
www.ohen.org

2. Oregon Christian Home Education Association Network (OCEAN)
17985 Falls City Rd., Dallas, OR 97338
Message line: (503) 288-1285
oceanet@oceanetwork.org
www.oceanetwork.org

3. LDS - Oregon Home Educators Association (LDS-OHEA)
www.lds-ohea.org
Conventions: #2 and #3 sponsor annual conferences; check the websites for updates.

Pennsylvania

There are three ways to "homeschool" here: parents at home, private professional tutor, or establishment of a homeschool as an extension of a church school. For parents to be qualified to teach, they must have a high school diploma or the equivalent. We are addressing the parent-taught option here. (If you are moving to Pennsylvania, please see the "Cautionary Words" on the PHEA website.)

Reporting: The parents must keep a portfolio of the materials used to teach, the work accomplished, and the results from standardized tests administered in grades 3, 5, and 8. A written assessment must be completed by June 30 of each year as well.

Compulsory Attendance: Ages eight to seventeen. Elementary: 900 hours per year; high school: 990 hours per year.

Required Subjects: Grades 1–8: arithmetic, reading, English spelling, writing, U.S. and Pennsylvania history, health and physiology, civics, physical education, art, music, geography, fire safety, general safety, and science. Grades 9–12: add English, literature, speech and writing (composition), world history, algebra, and geometry.

Testing: As just noted, standardized tests must be administered in grades 3, 5, and 8.

State Organizations:

1. Catholic Homeschoolers of PA
101 South College St., Myerstown, PA 17067
717-866-5425
info@catholichomeschoolpa.org
www.catholichomeschoolpa.org

2. The Christian Homeschool Association of Penn (CHAP)
CHAP 2710 N. Colebrook Rd. Manheim, PA 17545
717-838-0980
www.chaponline.com

3. Penn Home Education Network (PHEN) (secular)
info@phen.org
www.phen.org

4. Pennsylvania Home Educators Association (PHEA)
401 Lincoln Ave., Pittsburgh, PA 15202
www.phea.net
Conventions: #1 and #2 sponsor annual conventions; check the websites for updates.

Rhode Island

This state requires parents to obtain prior permission to homeschool from the local school board and to meet that board's requirements for the home school.

Reporting: Attendance records must be kept and submitted to the local school officials when requested. The number of days of attendance required is not specified, but must be equal to the public schools. (Be sure to find this out for yourself before proceeding.)

Compulsory Attendance: Ages six to sixteen.

Required Subjects: Arithmetic, reading, writing, English skills, geography, U.S. and state history and government (in grade 4), physical education, and health; in high school, U.S. government and the Constitution are added.

Testing: An annual assessment can be required. However, the law provides that the parents can choose what type of assessment will be used.

State Organization:

Rhode Island Guild of Home Teachers (RIGHT)
P.O. Box 432, Coventry, RI 02816
www.rihomeschool.com

South Carolina

This state recognizes three ways to homeschool. The first is based on the approval of the local school district, the second is to establish a home-school under the auspices of the South Carolina Association of Independent Homeschools, and the third is to establish a homeschool under the auspices of a homeschool association with at least fifty members. All three require the parent to possess at least a high school diploma or GED. In other requirements, all are virtually the same.

Reporting: Parents must maintain a record of subjects taught, a portfolio of the child's work, activities the child has engaged in, a record of the academic assessments, and a semi annual progress report.

Compulsory Attendance: Ages five to seventeen or high school graduation; 180 days per year, 4.5 hours per day, for 810 hours per year.

Required Subjects: Math, reading, writing, literature and English composition in grades 7–12, science, and social studies.

Testing: The student must fulfill the annual statewide testing requirements.

State Organizations:

1. Academic Advantage Association
P.O. Box 806, Lyman, SC 29365
864-968-1118
info@aaa-sc.com
www.aaa-sc.com

2. Carolina Homeschooler
P.O. Box 1421, Lancaster, SC 29721
editor@carolinahomeschooler.com
www.carolinahomeschooler.com

South Dakota

Reporting: Parents must submit to the state Department of Education a notice of intent form to the local superintendent. It must be notarized, and if it is the first-time filing, must be accompanied by the child's birth certificate or a sworn statement of identification. A copy of the child's birth certificate must be kept at home.

Compulsory Attendance: Ages seven to sixteen; nine-month school year.

Required Subjects: Math and language arts (typically, reading, writing, spelling, grammar, punctuation, comprehension).

Testing: Standardized tests must be administered in grades 2, 4, 8, and 11, and the results must show satisfactory progress.

State Organizations:

1. Alternative Instruction Association of S. Dakota (AIA) (religious and nonreligious)
14720 Home Place, Sturgis, SD 57785
www.geocities.com/aia_cc

2. S. Dakota Christian Home Educators (SDCHE)
P.O. Box 9571, Rapid City, SD 57709
SDCHE@sdche.org
www.sdche.org/contact.html

Tennessee

Parents have three options for homeschooling:

1. Be a homeschool as an individual family.
2. Be a homeschool as part of a church school.
3. Operate as an extension campus of a church school.

Option 3 has the fewest requirements; Option 1 has the most. Those will be listed here. Parents who are teaching grades K–8 need only a high school diploma or equivalent. To teach grades 9–12, either a bachelor's degree or a waiver from the education commissioner is required.

Reporting: Parents must file a notice of intent to the local school superintendent by August 1 of each year. Attendance records must be kept and submitted to the local superintendent at the end of each school year.

Compulsory Attendance: Ages six to seventeen; 180 days per year, four hours per day.

Required Subjects: For grades K–8, no requirements. For grades 9–12, the parents must teach either a college prep track, per the guidelines of the state four-year colleges, or a general studies track, per the requirements of the state board of education, to achieve high school graduation.

Testing: Parents must arrange for a standardized test to be administered by the commissioner of education in grades 5, 7, and 9.

State Organizations:

1. Tennessee Home Education Association (Christian)
3677 Richbriar Court, Nashville, TN 37211
615-834-3529
jcthornton3@earthlink.net
http://tnhea.org

2. TnHomeEd.com (Christian)
info@TnHomeEd.com
www.tnhomeed.com
Convention: Memphis Home Education Association (MHEA) Conference and Curriculum Fair, Memphis, Tennessee; for information see their website, www.memphishomeed.org.

Texas

Here parents operate their homeschool with the same status as a private school. They have complete freedom to regulate themselves.

Compulsory Attendance: Ages six to eighteen; no daily attendance required.
Required Subjects: Math, reading, spelling, grammar, and citizenship.

State Organizations:

Texas Homeschool Coalition
P.O. Box 6747, Lubbock, TX 79493
ph. 806-744-4441; fax 806-744-4446
staff@thsc.org
www.thsc.org
Conventions: For all of these events, please see the respective websites for updates.

1. Rethinking Education Annual Conference (secular)
www.rethinkingeducation.com

2. Texas Homeschool Coalition Conference (Christian)
www.thsc.org/convention

3. Homeschool FEAST (Christian)
www.homeschoolfeast.com/bookfair/Bookfairhome.htm

4. ARCH Catholic Conference
www.arch-homeschool.org/wst_page4.html

Utah

Here parents have two options: they can give notice to the school board of their individual homeschool program, or they can form a private school with other homeschooling families. No qualification for teaching is set forth, but the local school board can determine ability to teach.

Reporting: Parents are required to give notice to the local school board.

Compulsory Attendance: Ages six to eighteen; same daily as public schools.

Required Subjects: The basic core curriculum of the public schools.

State Organization:

Utah Home Education Association (UHEA)

www.uhea.org

Convention: UHEA sponsors an annual conference; check the website for updates.

Vermont

This state has the following specific requirements for parents to follow:

Reporting: There is no attendance reporting requirement, although the state requires 175 days of instruction. The parents must file a written notice with the Education Commissioner on or after March 1 for the coming year.

Parents also have to turn in an annual assessment in one of the following forms: (1) an assessment from a state-approved school teacher, (2) a report from a (boxed) curriculum provider along with the family's own portfolio of the child's work, or (3) the results of an accepted standardized test, administered according to the state-approved guidelines—usually by a librarian, teacher, or other similar third party.

Compulsory Attendance: Ages six to sixteen with some broad exceptions.

Required Subjects: Math, reading, writing, English, U.S. and state history, citizenship, physical education, American literature, science, and the arts.

Testing: As indicated under "Reporting" requirements.

State Organizations:

1. Vermont Association of Home Educators

vahemail@afo.net

www.vermonthomeschool.org

2. Vermont Home Education Network

P.O. Box 255, Woodbury, VT 05681

info@vhen.net

www.vhen.net

Virginia

Parents have three options for not having their children enrolled in public schools: (1) operate a homeschool, (2) operate a homeschool under the state religious exemption, or (3) hire a private tutor who is a certified teacher. The parent who uses the first option must have a high school diploma, be a certified teacher, or use an approved correspondence course.

Reporting: Parents must file an annual notice of intent with the local superintendent of education by August 15. If moving into the district, then the parents should file the notice as soon as is reasonable and then comply with any other requirements within thirty days of that time.

Compulsory Attendance: Ages five to eighteen.

Testing: Parents must administer a standardized test or some equivalent evaluation each year and submit the results to the local superintendent by August 1.

State Organizations:

1. Home Education Association of Virginia (HEAV)
2248 G Dabney Road, Richmond, Virginia, 23230
804-278-9200
info@heav.org.
http://heav.org

2. The Organization of Virginia Homeschoolers
P.O. Box 5131, Charlottesville, VA 22905
866-513-6173
info@vahomeschoolers.org
www.vahomeschoolers.org

Conventions: #1 sponsors an annual conference; check the website for updates.

Washington

This state offers two methods for homeschooling: parents teach at home independently or else as part of an approved private school for home education. The qualifications for teaching are rather strict: be supervised by a teacher, have completed forty-five college hours, or be approved by the local superintendent.

Reporting: Parents must file an annual notice of intent by September 15 or within two weeks of the beginning of a public school quarter. Parents must maintain the child's standardized test scores, academic progress assessments, and records of immunizations.

Compulsory Attendance: Ages eight to eighteen; 1,000 hours per year, which is 5.5 hours per day for 180 days.

Required Subjects: Math, reading, writing, spelling, language skills, science, social studies, history, music, art, and health.

Testing: An annual standardized test must be administered by a state-qualified person, or the child must be evaluated by a working teacher.

State Organizations:

1. Washington Homeschool Organization (WHO)
6632 S. 191st Place, Ste. E100, Kent, WA 98032
Message: 425-251-0439
WHOoffice@foxinternet.net
www.washhomeschool.org

2. Washington Natural Learners Association
34 E Monks Rd., Camano Island, WA 98282
360-387-7537
wanaturallearnasc@verizon.net
http://wnla.tripod.com
Conventions:
WHO Annual Conference: check website for updates.
Christian Heritage Home Educators of Washington: check www.christian
   heritageonline.org/events/2007-christian-heritage-conference.

West Virginia

Parents must possess a high school diploma to homeschool.

Reporting: Parents must file a notice of intent two weeks before beginning to teach.

Compulsory Attendance: Ages six to sixteen.

Required Subjects: None are specified, but the child must be assessed in the subjects of math, reading, language, social studies, and science.

Testing: Parents must either administer a standardized test, have their child's portfolio evaluated by a certified teacher, participate in the state testing program, or have their child's progress evaluated by some other means approved by the local school superintendent.

State Organizations:

1. Christian Home Educators of West Virginia (CHEWV)
administrator@chewv.org
www.chewv.org

2. West Virginia Home Educators Association
P.O. Box 3707, Charleston, WV. 25337-3707
800-736-9843
www.wvhea.org

Convention: #1 sponsors an annual conference; check the website for updates.

Wisconsin

Here a homeschool is referred to as a *home-based private educational program.* Parents do not have to qualify to teach their own.

Reporting: Parents must file a statement of enrollment with the state Department of Education by October 15 of each year.

Compulsory Attendance: Ages six to eighteen; 875 hours per year (4.86 hours per day for 180 days, for example.)

Required Subjects: Math, reading, language arts, science, health, and social studies.

State Organizations:

1. Wisconsin Christian Home Educators Association (WCHEA)
P.O. Box 320458, Franklin, WI 53132
jang@wisconsinchea.com
www.wisconsinchea.com

2. Wisconsin Parents Association (WPA)
P.O. Box 2502, Madison, WI 53701
Message: 608-283-3131
www.homeschooling-wpa.org
Conventions: Both groups sponsor annual conferences; check the websites for updates.

Wyoming

Parents are not required to qualify to teach their children.

Reporting: Each year, parents must submit a curriculum to the local board that shows that the child is receiving a basic academic program.

Compulsory Attendance: Ages seven to sixteen or completion of the tenth grade; 175 days per year.

Required Subjects: Math, reading, writing, literature, science, civics, and history.

State Organization:

Homeschoolers of Wyoming (HOW) (Christian; statement of faith required)
www.homeschoolersofwy.org
Convention: Sponsors annual convention; check the website for updates.

Appendix B: Where to Go for More Information

List B.1. Homeschooling Magazines, Print and Online

Just a few short years ago, this section would have contained only print magazines (see List B.1A). Now there are numerous online publications, with new ones seeming to spring up each month (see List B.1B). Both media provide excellent information for homeschoolers.

List B.1A. Print Publications

- *Home Education Magazine.* Founded in 1983, *HEM* is the oldest active publication in homeschooling and is likely the most popular in the strictly nonreligious homeschooling world. *HEM* offers articles and features by homeschooling parents, covering nearly every topic of interest to secular homeschoolers. Subscription rate: $6.50 per copy; $32 per year (six issues), prepaid. P.O. Box 1083, Tonasket, WA 98855-1083; 509-486-1351; www.homeedmag.com.
- *Homeschooling Today. Homeschooling Today* is a Christian publication, serving the interests of Christian homeschoolers with regular articles, features, and reviews. Subscription rate: $6.99 per copy; $21.99 per year (six issues), prepaid. P.O. Box 836, Barker, TX 77413; 281-579-0033; http://homeschooltoday.com.
- *Life Learning Magazine. LLM* is edited by Wendy Priesnitz, a well-known Canadian homeschooling mom, author, and home-business expert. She has written nine books, including a popular home-business book *Bringing It Home: A Startup Guide for You and Your Family. LLM* subscription rates, prepaid, are one year personal (nonlibrary) (six issues) $27.00, two years personal (twelve issues) $51.00. c/o Life Media, P.O. Box 112, Niagara Falls, NY 14304-0112, or 508-264 Queens Quay W, Toronto, Ontario M5J 1B5; www.lifelearningmagazine.com.
- *Practical Homeschooling.* Published by Home Life, Inc., *PHS* was founded and is owned by Mary Pride, a well-known and popular author and reviewer in the Christian homeschooling world. Pride is the author of the well-known *Big Book of Home Learning. PHS* is one of the oldest Christian homeschooling publications and offers a broad variety of information and resources. The website also offers a catalog of various items for sale. Subscription rate: $6.95 per copy; $19.95 per year (six issues), prepaid. P.O. Box 1190, Fenton, MO 63026-1190; 800-346-6322 (10:00 to 4:00 Central Time, Monday through Friday) or 636-529-0137; svc@home-school.com; www.home-school.com.
- *Family Times.* Published by Home Educator, this newsletter is edited by Jane R. Boswell and features articles by a variety of people relating

to homeschooling. P.O. Box 6442, Brunswick, ME 04011; www. HomeEducator.com/FamilyTimes.

- *The Old Schoolhouse, LLC.* Originally published by Paul and Gena Suarez, now published by the Wuehler family, *TOS* is the "newest" Christian homeschool publication containing many features and articles of interest to Christian homeschoolers. The website also contains many features such as the Schoolhouse Store. Subscription rate: $27.95 prepaid one year (four issues). (Many package specials are shown on the website.) P.O. Box 10, White Pine, Tennessee 37890; ph. and fax 888-718-HOME (888-718-4663); www.thehomeschoolmagazine.com.

- *Homeschool Enrichment Magazine.* This is a Christian publication of the Lewis family: Frank, Kari, Matthew, and Jonathan. *HSE* provides support, encouragement, and guidance to Christian homeschooling families or those interested in homeschooling. The Lewises seem to have a great deal of life experience and probably know whereof they speak. Regular subscription price is $21.97 for six issues, but the website offers discounts. P.O. Box 163, Pekin, IL 61555-0163; hello@ homeschoolenrichment.com.

- *The Link* Homeschool Newspaper. Published since 1995, *The Link* is the only national homeschooling publication that is all-inclusive, meaning that it caters to religious and nonreligious homeschoolers alike. Its articles are from both camps of homeschooling; its readers and advertisers definitely are. It is also the only national homeschool publication that is free of charge. *The Link* sponsors a conference in the Los Angeles area and publishes a free e-newsletter, *The Way Home*, as well as an online edition of the paper, with extensive information at its website. 587 N. Ventu Park Road, Ste. E-911, Newbury Park, CA 91320; 805-497-3311; general information: linkadvertising@verizon.net; editorial use: mary.thelink@verizon.net; www.homeschoolnewslink.com.

List B.1B. Online Publications

- *Classical Homeschooling Magazine.* This unique publication actually exists in hard copy, but only four issues are available; the website has continuous news and information about the classical method of homeschooling, including the Great Books, important conferences, the ideal university, the true liberal arts, and much more. P.O. Box 10726, Bainbridge Island, WA 98110; www.classicalhomeschooling.com.

- *EHO Lite.* This is a Christian online publication with many pages of resources, advice, and ideas especially for new homeschooling families. 707 Vestal St., Woodbridge, VA 22191; 703-953-7632; editor@eho.org;http://eho.org.

- *Everything Homeschooling.* This is a monthly online magazine devoted to, well, everything homeschooling! In addition to twelve issues per year, there are daily and weekly updates, lesson suggestions, activities for all age levels, advice, resources—everything for the homeschooling family. www.everythinghomeschooling.com.

- *The Way Home* e-newsletter. This is a free, weekly email newsletter published by *The Link* Homeschool Newspaper, containing excellent articles by John Taylor Gatto, Dr. Mary Hood, homeschooling parents, and other regular columnists for *The Link*, as well as product coupons, recipes, regular features of interest, and resources that are valuable to homeschoolers. Subscribe at www.homeschoolnewslink.com.

- *The Utmost Way.* A Christian online magazine with many diverse articles and resources of interest to families who wish to make home the central location for their living, with homeschooling a part of this, of course. Many excellent free resources and information. www.utmost-way.com/maincontents.htm.

List B.2. Books for Homeschoolers

This is not an exhaustive list, as there are many, many excellent books on homeschooling, or aspects of it, that come and go. Many of the out-of-print books on List B.2B are still available from Amazon, Alibris, and undoubtedly from other sources. Homeschoolers tend to recycle books so that others may enjoy them. You can even find them in some libraries.

List B.2A. In-Print Books About Homeschooling and Child Learning

- *Carschooling: Over 350 Entertaining Games and Activities to Turn Travel Time into Learning Time,* by Diane Flynn Keith. Keith developed this idea to keep her children gainfully occupied during long hours in the car. This mobile classroom approach is one of the best things about homeschooling—you can always be taking in information! You can obtain an autographed copy of this excellent, useful, and fun book from Keith at www.carschooling.com.
- *From Homeschool to College and Work,* by Alison McKee This book is the up-to-date essential tome on "What's a homeschooler to do after high school?" McKee's two grown children have successfully gone on to college and adulthood, and she passes along her knowledge about college entrance and other issues. (The Sample Transcript for College Entrance in Appendix D of this book is taken from McKee's book; please see Appendix E for a valuable discount coupon.)
- *Books by Dr. Raymond and Dorothy Moore.* The Moores, along with John Holt, were the pioneers of modern homeschooling from the educator's point of view. Unlike Holt, the Moores had children whom they homeschooled. As professionals, they encouraged parents to home-school, to consider "schooling" to be a regular part of parenting, and to not apply pressure to young children to learn to read and do other academic subjects. Their books include *Better Late Than Early* and its scholarly version, *School Can Wait II.* The Moores' research demonstrated that children who learned to read "later" suffered no long-term ill effects; in fact, at the age of eleven or twelve they could read on par with those who had learned to read earlier. In addition to these two classics of homeschooling, many other books by the Moores are available at their Foundation's website, www.moorefoundation.com. P.O. Box 98, North Bonneville, WA 98639; 509-427-7779.
- *Books by David and Micki Colfax. Hard Times in Paradise* and *Homeschooling for Excellence: How to Take Charge of Your Child's Education – And Why You Absolutely Must.* David Colfax was a university professor in the Midwest. He left academia in the early 1970s,

to move his wife, Micki, and their four young sons to Boonville, California, to start a new life. On forty-seven acres of rugged mountaintop, without running water, phone service, or electricity, they built a house and ultimately raised goats for a living. They homeschooled the boys, who all successfully attended Ivy League schools and have gone on to professional success. Thus the Colfaxes became the "poster family" for homeschooling in the early years of its modern incarnation. When someone would ask a homeschooling family about college entrance or admission viability, the Colfax family's story could be cited as a successful example. Their experiences and advice are still timely, and both books provide wonderful support in the "dark hours" of homeschooling, when you wonder if you can *really* do this.

- *The Teenage Liberation Handbook: How to Quit School and Get a Real Life and Education*, by Grace Llewellyn (www.lowryhousepublishers. com/TeenageLiberationHandbook.htm). This book is a landmark in the field of homeschooling. The teen years can be fraught with difficulties because so many families use the public school socialization as their model, and it simply does not fit a homeschooled teenager. Llewellyn recognized this long ago and developed her book to assist in this very important area of child-rearing and homeschooling.

- *Books by John Taylor Gatto.* Gatto is one of the most intelligent and interesting voices in the world of alternative education—the official category that homeschooling falls into. Gatto retired from his job as a junior high school teacher in Manhattan and immediately set about writing and lecturing about the need to abandon the school system he had been a part of for thirty years. In *Dumbing Us Down*, he asserted that there can be no reform of a system that is broken beyond repair, and that homeschooling—a return to the original way the American colonials raised their children—is the ultimate answer to the ills of public schools that he has witnessed all of his life. This book addresses how the system has repeatedly reduced the intellectual level of students to the point of creating a virtual thinking and knowledge crisis in America. The original of the book is no longer in print, but the publisher released a tenth anniversary edition in 2002, with 20 percent more text than the original. *The Exhausted School* is the transcript of a live show presented at Carnegie Hall in November 1991. Gatto organized the event, which consisted of four of his former pupils reminiscing about what had been significant in their educations and four directors of alternative educational institutions discussing what they did differently from public schools. In his massive tome *The Underground History of American Education*, Gatto traces the development of American institutional education from the first compulsory school edict in Plymouth, Massachusetts, to today's "No Child Left Behind" legislation. He provides not only the timeline aspects, but also the underlying social engineering agendas of various individuals and groups in the growth of mandatory schooling. Please see Gatto's website for many more titles as well as CD-ROMs of speeches and interviews. www.johntaylorgatto.com/book store/index.htm.

- *100 Top Picks for Homeschool Curriculum: Choosing the Right Curriculum and Approach for Your Child's Learning Style*, by Cathy Duffy. Duffy has been an expert in curriculum choices and homeschool teaching products for more than fifteen years. She has been advising parents on products in her many well-written books, and the latest one is another excellent addition to her line. www.cathyduffyreviews.com.

List B.2B. Out-of-Print Homeschooling Books

These books have served the homeschooling world for many years. They are no longer available brand new, but can be purchased used from Alibris or Amazon. Many are still in public libraries as well.

- *Books by John Holt. How Children Learn* (Holt Publishers); *How Children Fail* (Holt Publishers). These seminal books by the late pioneer of unschooling are worth having, as it is edifying to take in Holt's unique thoughts firsthand.
- *Books by Linda Dobson. Homeschooling – The Early Years: Your Complete Guide to Successfully Homeschooling the 3- to 8-Year-Old Child; The Ultimate Book of Homeschooling Ideas; The First Year of Homeschooling Your Child.* Dobson is one of the most prolific and helpful authors in homeschooling. She has written many other books, as an Internet search on her name will reveal. All of these and many more Dobson tomes can be found from used-book sellers and are worth reading and referring to.
- *Books by Rebecca Rupp. The Complete Home Learning Source Book; Home Learning Year Year.* Rupp is in the same category as Linda Dobson, having written many, many books that are either about homeschooling or useful to homeschoolers. Search for her name on the Internet and you will see an abundance of very useful books, published in the mid-1990s and all available used.
- *The Homeschooling Almanac 2000–2001 and 2002–2003*, by Mary and Michael Leppert. The legal information is outdated and the coupons are long expired; however, the core material of the *Almanac* remains valuable and useful. It covers all of the pitfalls faced by prospective homeschooling families, beginners, and even "old hands" who reach a sticking point. The product comments offer excellent advice and information. Many used copies are available at reasonable prices, as well as in some public libraries.
- *Books by Mary Griffith. The Homeschooling Handbook; From Preschool to High School: A Parent's Guide; The Unschooling Handbook: How to Use the Whole World As Your Child's Classroom.* These two books are also long out of print, but still contain vital and useful information for homeschooling parents—both current and prospective. The core ideas of teaching one's own children do not change over time.
- *And What About College? How Homeschooling Can Lead to Admissions to the Best Colleges and Universities*, by Cafi Cohen. Cohen homeschooled her children through high school and into college. Her son attended the Air Force Academy and was accepted based on Cohen's

homemade transcripts. Although much of the college and university information may no longer be current, the transcript and record-keeping advice is vital and helps put a parent's mind at ease.

- *Government Nannies: The Cradle-to-Grave Agenda of Goals 2000 and Outcome Based Education,* by Cathy Duffy, with a foreword by John Taylor Gatto (Noble Publishing). Of course, now "Goals 2000" sounds as quaint as "1984," but in 1995, when this book was published, such a draconian federal government program loomed large in threatening the sovereignty of the family—which would likely have resulted in a death blow to homeschooling "rights" everywhere. Not only is this book still timely because of the likelihood of future programs much like Goals 2000, but the foreword by Gatto is a classic in its own right. Available used at www.christianbook.com.
- *The Continuum Concept,* by Jean Liedloff. Liedloff spent two-and-a-half years living with South American Indians in a primitive state. Her observations of their child-rearing customs and practices are eye-opening for U.S. parents, especially those involved in homeschooling.

Appendix C: Who's Who in Homeschooling

This is a by no means exhaustive list of people who come up in homeschooling conversations. The list is meant to serve the beginning homeschooling parent who is "considering it" and not yet familiar with these people, but may want to be.

Albert, David H. A proponent of unschooling; a well-known homeschooling dad, author, and conference speaker; and the original publisher of John Taylor Gatto's seminal book, *Dumbing Us Down*. Albert has written regularly for *The Link* Homeschool Newspaper and *Home Education Magazine*, and his articles have appeared in many other publications all over the world. He lives in Olympia, Washington, homeschooling his younger daughter with his wife, Ellen. Among his books are *And the Skylark Sings with Me*, *Adventures in Homeschooling and Community-Based Education*, and *Homeschooling and the Voyage of Self-Discovery*.

Andreola, Karen. A homeschooling mom, author, Charlotte Mason columnist, and all-around expert on the Charlotte Mason method.

Andreola learned about the Mason Method firsthand through of her own use of it with her family and then began researching and writing about it for others. She founded and owns the Charlotte Mason Research and Supply Company, which provides interesting ancillary products and services to those interested in the CM method. She writes a regular Mason column in the Christian magazine *Practical Homeschooling*, and her book *The Charlotte Mason Companion* is very popular.

Beechick, Ruth. Author of the books *An Easy Start in Arithmetic, A Home Start in Reading, Language and Thinking for Young Children, You Can Teach Your Child Successfully*, and *A Strong Start in Language.* She is also a popular speaker.

Blumenfeld, Sam. Author of eight books on the topic of education, including *Is Public Education Necessary?* which contains an excellent history of public education in America. He is also the creator of the reading program Alpha Phonics and a popular teacher and speaker.

Cohen, Cafi. A homeschool mother, columnist, and author of *What About College?* discussing college admissions for homeschoolers. She also authored many books for Prima Publishing in the late 1990s and early 2000s. Cohen is no longer an active homeschooler, but her books provide sound advice and insight into homeschooling high school children and college entrance matters.

Colfax, David and Micki. A couple who homeschooled their four boys on a goat farm in Northern California in the early 1980s and attained national attention as their first son (and subsequently three others) was accepted at Harvard and Yale. They are the authors of two books on homeschooling: *Home Schooling for Excellence* and *Hard Times in Paradise.*

Dobson, Linda. Homeschooling mother and popular speaker, she also writes regularly for *Home Education Magazine*. Dobson is the author of numerous books, including *The Art of Education, The Homeschooling Book of Answers, Homeschooling – The Early Years*, and *Homeschoolers' Success Stories.* She is also active in the Organization of VA Homeschoolers, www.vahomeschoolers.org, which represents the interests of all homeschoolers in Virginia.

Dodd, Sandra. Homeschooling mother of three and a lifelong proponent of unschooling. She has written about it for *Home Education Magazine* and elsewhere. She is also a popular speaker at conferences and her website, http://sandradodd.com, is very informative.

Duffy, Cathy. Veteran Christian homeschooling mother and author of the Christian Home Educators' Curriculum Manuals, which provide extensive product information, and the widely acclaimed book *Government Nannies*, which detailed the government's effort to extend its influence over the home and family through its Goals 2000 public school program. Even though Goals 2000 came and went, the fundamental ideas are still alive in government circles, and the book is significant in providing a view inside bureaucratic planning that may reappear in the future. Duffy is also a much sought after conference speaker. http://www.cathyduffyreviews.com.

Farenga, Pat. President of Holt Associates. Along with his wife, Day, Farenga has homeschooled their three daughters, all of whom are nearly finished with homeschooling. He also coordinates and sponsors the annual Growing Without Schooling conference in the Boston area. He is a frequent speaker at conferences nationwide and is one of the most esteemed unschoolers in the field, having worked closely with John Holt for many years and carried on Holt's support of unschooling. See his website, http://www.patfarenga.com, for new information.

Farris, Mike. President and founder of the Home School Legal Defense Association (HSLDA) and one of its lead attorneys. He is also chancellor of Patrick Henry College, a leading family advocate in Washington, The author of thirteen books, and a homeschooling father of ten children and grandfather of seven. He and his wife began homeschooling in 1982. www.hslda.org.

Gardner, Howard. Harvard psychologist who discovered, researched, and wrote about the seven intelligences all humans possess. This in turn led to more research about the different learning styles we all share.

Gatto, John Taylor. A thirty-year veteran teacher of Manhattan public junior high schools and three-time winner of the New York City and New York State Teacher of the Year award; education reformer, thinker, and author of many books about public education and life, including *Dumbing Us Down, The Underground History of Education in America, The Empty Child,* and many more. See www.johntaylorgatto.com for more.

Harris, Greg. Homeschooling father, author, and popular conference speaker. Author of *The Christian Homeschool* and other books.

Hegener, Mark and Helen. Parents of five exclusively homeschooled children and founders and publishers of *Home Education Magazine.* They also are frequent conference speakers.

Holt, John. The late pioneering researcher, teacher, and founder of *Growing Without Schooling* magazine in Boston. Holt coined the term *unschooling* and authored many books about children and learning.

Hood, Dr. Mary. A veteran Christian homeschooling mother with a Ph.D. in education. She and her husband have homeschooled their five children for fifteen years. She is the author of several books, including *The Relaxed Homeschool* and *The Joyful Homeschooler,* and has written a series of guidebooks for homeschoolers, *Relaxed Recordkeeping* and *Helping Children Learn to Write.* Dr. Hood's excellent sense of humor and casual approach allow her to put even the most stressed-out parent at ease. She is a popular conference speaker and editor of *The Relaxed HomeSchooler* newsletter. Her website is www.archersforthelord.com.

Kaseman, Larry and Susan. Homeschooling parents of four and authors of *Taking Charge Through Homeschooling: Personal and Political Empowerment.* They write regularly for *Home Education Magazine.*

Keith, Diane Flynn. Homeschooling mother of two grown sons; editor and publisher of *Homefires: A Journal of Homeschooling;* author of the Prima book *Carschooling,* and the founder and moderator of Clickschooling, a popular online resource for educational resources and ideas. Keith is also a very popular conference lecturer. She is also an opponent of universal preschooling. www.homefires.com.

Hodson, Victoria Kindle, M.A. Author of many books; coauthor of *Discover Your Child's Learning Styles.* Consultant and co-owner of Reflective Educational Perspectives, a learning styles consultation firm in Ventura, California. Hodson is a popular conference workshop presenter. LearningSuccess Institute; info@learningsuccesscoach.com.

Klicka, Chris. Senior counsel for HSLDA since 1985, homeschool father of seven, and author of *The Right Choice: The Incredible Failure of Public Education, The Rising Hope of Homeschooling, The Right to Homeschool: A Guide to the Law on Parents' Rights in Education,* and *Homeschooling in the United States: A Statutory Analysis.*

Leppert, Mary and Michael. Publishers of *The Link* Homeschool Newspaper, producers of *The Link* "kid comfortable" Homeschooling Conferences, producers of *The Way Home* e-newsletter, producers of *Autonomous Parenting* e-newsletters. Authors of homeschooling books.

Levison, Catherine. Ten-plus-year expert on the Charlotte Mason method, through her research and application with her own five children—all of whom are completely homeschooled. Levison has written a number of popular books about the Mason approach, including *A Charlotte Mason Education* and its sequel, *More Charlotte Mason Education,* which are very clear how-to manuals for applying Charlotte Mason's techniques and philosophy. She also writes a regular Charlotte Mason column for both editions of *The Link* Homeschool Newspaper and is a very popular speaker at *The Link* "kid comfortable" Homeschool Conferences and many other conferences and shows around the country.

Llewellyn, Grace. A homeschooled adult, Llewellyn is the author of *The Teenage Liberation Handbook: How to Quit School and Get a Real Life and Education.* She also writes for various homeschool publications.

Mann, Horace (1776–1859). Instrumental in establishing the public school elementary system in Massachusetts, which later served as a model for the United States system. His efforts provided a setback to parents' rights to educate their own children. He helped assemble the first state board of education and was its secretary for more than ten years. Mann served on the Massachusetts state legislature and was later elected to the House of Representatives, where he was an aggressive advocate for public education (versus homeschooling). Mann was the president of Antioch College in Ohio from 1853 until he died in 1859.

Mason, Charlotte (1842–1923). British educator during the Victorian period, who was homeschooled herself and later became an advocate for homeschooling or private schools with very much parental involvement. Her method (see List 2.2, The Charlotte Mason Method) is one of the most popular in modern homeschooling.

McKee, Allison. Homeschooling mother of two grown children and author of *From Homeschool to College and Work.* McKee is also a proponent of unschooling and frequently writes on the topic for various homeschooling publications. www.bittersweethouse.com.

Moore, Dr. Raymond and Dorothy. Parents of two partially homeschooled children and the developers of the Moore method of homeschooling. They were pioneers in the homeschooling movement and responsible for many of the pro-homeschooling laws in California. They authored *Better Late Than Early, School Can Wait, Home Grown Kids, Home Spun Schools, Home Built Discipline, Home Made Help, Minding Your Own Business,* and *The Successful Family Handbook.*

Neill, A. S. Founder and headmaster of Summerhill School in England and author of the 1960 book *Summerhill: A Radical Approach to Child Rearing,* which has influenced homeschooling parents with its radical findings on how children learn and what stops them from learning.

Pelullo-Willis, Mariaemma. Popular homeschool consultant and co-owner of Reflective Educational Perspectives. Author of *What to Do When They Don't Get It* and *Homeschooling the Child with Learning Problems,* and coauthor of

Discover Your Child's Learning Style. Pelullo-Willis is a popular conference workshop presenter, along with her partner, Victoria Kindle-Hodson. LearningSuccess Institute; info@learningsuccesscoach.com.

Pride, Mary. Publisher of the popular Christian homeschool magazine *Practical Homeschooling.* Author of *The Big Book of Home Learning, The Way Home, All the Way Home, Schoolproof,* and *The Child Abuse Industry,* and coauthor of both *The Unholy Sacrifices of the New Age* and *Ancient Empires of the New Age.*

Priesnitz, Wendy. Canadian homeschooling mother, advocate, speaker, and author of the book *School Free: The Homeschooling Handbook.* She is also recognized as a home-business expert. Priesnitz has authored eight other books, including *Bringing It Home: A Startup Guide for You and Your Family.*

Rousseau, Jean-Jacques. Eighteenth-century French philosopher and writer who inadvertently influenced educators with his book *Emile* (1762), which ultimately led to both public school and unschooling.

Rupp, Rebecca. Homeschooling mother of three and author of several books, including *Everything You Never Learned About Birds, Good Stuff, Committed to Memory, The Dragon of Lonely Island, The Complete Home Learning Source Book,* and *Getting Started in Homeschooling.* She is also a regular columnist for *Home Education Magazine.*

Appendix D: Sample Transcript for College Admission

The following is a nonsequential excerpt from the insightful book *From Homeschool to College and Work*, 3rd edition, by Alison McKee, published by Bittersweet House, copyright 1997, 1998, 2004. Used by permission. Available from Bittersweet House, P.O. Box 5211, Madison, WI 53705-5211.

Alison McKee's homeschooled son, Christian, applied to various colleges using a narrative transcript, portions of which are excerpted here. To see the entire transcript and obtain other pertinent advice, please see *From Homeschool to College and Work*. As McKee mentions in the book, although Christian included a query letter, after all was said and done he felt that it was unnecessary; indeed, Alison feels that as homeschooling has become more

---

commonplace than it was when he was applying, it is now so widely accepted that such letters are unnecessary or even counterproductive. Incidentally, Christian was accepted at a number of schools, including the University of Minnesota, Minneapolis; University of Wisconsin, Eau Claire; and University of Wisconsin, Madison. He ultimately attended Kalamazoo College (his first choice) on a nearly full scholarship. (For more about transcripts, please refer to Lists 5.1 and 5.2.)

. . . Another admissions officer praised the thoroughness with which we documented Christian's unusual learning exploits and mentioned that if other homeschoolers were as thorough in their work, the process of considering homeschooled applicants would be much less cumbersome for their admissions committees.

This narrative transcript is an effort to document Christian's life in terms that are relevant to traditional academic categories or subject areas. We have drawn primarily on the records of his work that have been kept by him and by us over the last 18 years. It describes a wide range of experiences at home, in the community and in traditional classroom settings. (*From Homeschool to College and Work,* Introduction)

English

The study of English, including reading, writing, speech and attendance at a wide variety of theatrical performances, has always been a natural part of Christian's life. Christian is widely read. Not only has he read for his own personal enjoyment but he has also read aloud to large live audiences and on the radio. Christian's writing experiences are many and varied. They include: Writing articles for various magazines, keeping a journal, letter and e-mail correspondence, writing research papers and writing radio copy. Christian has had public speaking experience. His experiences include speaking before the Wisconsin state legislature's Education Committee (at age 11), participation in many panel discussions, being an interviewee for both radio and T.V. reporters, speaking about education in University of Wisconsin teacher education classes, and as a teacher of both fly tying and German. As a young man with a wide variety of interests Christian has attended theatrical productions ranging from comedy to drama and musical productions.

Shakespearean Experiences

Plays Read	Plays Seen
• *The Taming of the Shrew*	*Macbeth*

A Sampling of Christian's Reading as It Related to the Study of English

Novels
Brent, *Incidents in the Life of a Slave Girl*
N. Maclean, *A River Runs Through It*

Short Stories
Garland, *The Return of a Private*
Poe, *Telltale Heart*

Plays
Guare, *Six Degrees of Separation*
Stoker, *Dracula*, the screenplay

Poetry
Beowulf
Eliot, *Four Quartets*

Essays
Orwell, *Politics and the English Language*

Writing

Samples of other types of writing Christian has engaged in are as follow:

Writing copy for live news broadcasts.

Video Studies

MacNeil, *The Story of English*

German

As a young boy, singing in the Madison (Wisconsin) Boy Choir, Christian went on many singing tours. In the summer of 1990 the Madison Boy Choir was invited to sing in Germany. To help keep costs for such a trip to a minimum, the boys stayed in German homes. As Christian's parents, we decided that Christian should learn some basic German so that he might be able to greet his hosts. Neither of us spoke German so in the summer of 1989 we enrolled him in the language immersion program offered by Concordia College of Moorhead, MN: Concordia Language Villages. [Note: For more on these, see List 3.6.] That two-week program was the beginning of Christian's study of German.

Concordia Language Villages

1989–1992 (age 11–14)   Concordia Language Villages German two-week camp program

1994 (age 16)   Concordia Language Villages Credit Abroad Program. Christian studied and worked in Germany for three weeks. He lived with a family in Wolffegg and commuted to Bad Waldsee by train for directed language study and work in a nursing home.

Tutorial Work, Traditional High School Work, College Classes

1989–1991   Private instruction

1991–1992   High School German 3 class

1994   Honors Introduction to Literature 284 at the University of Wisconsin, Madison

Science

(Note: Many people are concerned about homeschoolers not being able to get into college without access to science lab classes. Since Christian had no lab course work, and especially since a dean of college admissions at a small liberal arts college was so impressed with this particular aspect of Christian's portfolio, I've decided to include the entire contents of this part of his portfolio. I hope that this will encourage other homeschoolers to let go of their worries about traditional course work and simply enjoy learning. Christian's first lab class came later on, it was a college course, and he managed to get an A without much difficulty.)

One of the philosophies that has guided our homeschooling has been that children are better able to learn when immersed in studies which have particular interest to them. As a result of our belief in this child-directed, rather than curriculum-directed approach to learning, Christian has not studied the sciences in a traditional manner. For example, as an eight-year-old, he was interested in dissection and thus dissected a frog, worm, crayfish, mussel and fetal pig . . . as a ten-year-old, he was fascinated with the nature preserve that is at our back door . . . he conducted an extensive habitat study of a particular portion of the park [that] included graphing temperature changes, recording numbers of particular species of birds present and recording and measuring the growth of particular grasses, trees and shrubs . . . he became acutely aware of the changes that took place in "his habitat." . . . his interests shifted to chemistry, so [he] took chemistry enrichment courses offered through . . . the University of Wisconsin and the Madison Public Schools. All of these studies were undertaken because of Christian's interest in the subject matter. His most intense scientific study, though, centered around trout fishing and fly tying and was carried out over a four-year period.

Entomology

Clarke & Goddard, *The Trout and The Fly*
Swischer & Richards, *Emergers*
Swischer & Richards, *Tying Hatch Simulator Flies*
LaFontaine, *Caddisflies*
Swischer, *Strategies for Selective Trout*
Schwiebert, *Nymphs*
Whitlock, *Fly Tiers Almanac*
Schweibert, *Trout*
Schweibert, *Matching the Hatch*
Whitlock, *Dave Whitlock's Guide to Aquatic Trout Foods*

Social Studies

World History

A Sampling of Literature Read
Gonick, *Cartoon History of the Universe I, II*
Schweibert, *Trout*

A Sampling of Videos Seen
Castle: PBS documentary
The Killing Fields
I, Claudius: PBS Masterpiece Theatre production
Schindler's List

American History

A Sampling of Literature Read
Brent, *Incidents in the Life of a Slave Girl*
Malcolm X, *The Autobiography of Malcolm X*

A Sampling of Videos Seen
History of Rock n' Roll: PBS documentary
Malcolm X: Making It Plain

A Sampling of Participatory Events
1992 and 1993   Participated in YMCA Youth in Government program
1994   Lived in Germany for three weeks with a German family
1996   Campaign volunteer for Dane County Board candidate, Ben Manske

Volunteer Work

Radio Work

1992–1994   Volunteer at WORT – a listener-sponsored, volunteer run, community radio station engineers taped shows (age 14–16). Pre-production work including pre-programming satellite de-modulators and taping carts for public service announcements.

1996   Elected to the Board of Directors, Badger Fly Fishers

1992   Campaign volunteer for U.S. Congressional candidate Ada Deer

(Attached to these pages of Christian's portfolio was a letter of recommendation for a study abroad program written by one of Christian's volunteer supervisors.)

By this point, the reader will notice that some of the book titles in Christian's transcript were used for more than one entry and that some of the entries were relatively sparse. In other words, overkill was not necessary. For the complete format the McKees used, please see Alison's book, which includes the title page with contact information and a brief Background and Philosophy section preceding the actual transcript; these quickly enabled admissions officers to understand where the McKees were coming from in educating their son.

Having outside verification of studies helps in the transcript creation; and letters of recommendation, particularly when supporting a coinciding detailed entry, are also very helpful to college admissions officers.

Appendix E:
Coupons

Bonnie Terry Learning

- Use original coupon; no photocopies permitted.
- Valid for one use only.
- Check with company for any shipping & handling costs.
- May not be combined with any other offer.

Literacy Unlimited

- Use original coupon; no photocopies permitted.
- Valid for one use only.
- Check with company for any shipping & handling costs.
- May not be combined with any other offer.

Bonnie Terry Learning

- Use original coupon; no photocopies permitted.
- Valid for one use only.
- Check with company for any shipping & handling costs.
- May not be combined with any other offer.

Bonnie Terry Learning

- Use original coupon; no photocopies permitted.
- Valid for one use only.
- Check with company for any shipping & handling costs.
- May not be combined with any other offer.

Davidson's Music

- Use original coupon; no photocopies permitted.
- Valid for one use only.
- Check with company for any shipping & handling costs.
- May not be combined with any other offer.

Ace Reader Pro Ace Reader Pro Deluxe

- Use original coupon; no photocopies permitted.
- Valid for one use only.
- Check with company for any shipping & handling costs.
- May not be combined with any other offer.

Evaluation Institute

- Use original coupon; no photocopies permitted.
- Valid for one use only.
- Check with company for any shipping & handling costs.
- May not be combined with any other offer.

Design-A-Study

- Use original coupon; no photocopies permitted.
- Valid for one use only.
- Check with company for any shipping & handling costs.
- May not be combined with any other offer.

Sound Reading Solutions

- Use original coupon; no photocopies permitted.
- Valid for one use only.
- Check with company for any shipping & handling costs.
- May not be combined with any other offer.

Cotton's Journey
a field trip in a box

- Use original coupon; no photocopies permitted.
- Valid for one use only.
- Check with company for any shipping & handling costs.
- May not be combined with any other offer.
- Send brochure to:
  P.O. Box 55, Tranquility, CA 93668

Peterson Method

- Use original coupon; no photocopies permitted.
- Valid for one use only.
- Check with company for any shipping & handling costs.
- May not be combined with any other offer.

Drills, Skills and More

- Use original coupon; no photocopies permitted.
- Valid for one use only.
- Check with company for any shipping & handling costs.
- May not be combined with any other offer.

Board Games Express

- Use original coupon; no photocopies permitted.
- Valid for one use only.
- Check with company for any shipping & handling costs.
- May not be combined with any other offer.

Drive Thru History: America

- Use original coupon; no photocopies permitted.
- Valid for one use only.
- Check with company for any shipping & handling costs.
- May not be combined with any other offer.

Kaybee Montessori

- Use original coupon; no photocopies permitted.
- Valid for one use only.
- Check with company for any shipping & handling costs.
- May not be combined with any other offer.

Home Science Adventures

- Use original coupon; no photocopies permitted.
- Valid for one use only.
- Check with company for any shipping & handling costs.
- May not be combined with any other offer.

Gordon School of Art

- Use original coupon; no photocopies permitted.
- Valid for one use only.
- Check with company for any shipping & handling costs.
- May not be combined with any other offer.

New Child Montessori

- Use original coupon; no photocopies permitted.
- Valid for one use only.
- Check with company for any shipping & handling costs.
- May not be combined with any other offer.

Guitar Lessons Interactive

- Use original coupon; no photocopies permitted.
- Valid for one use only.
- Check with company for any shipping & handling costs.
- May not be combined with any other offer.

Canon Press

- Use original coupon; no photocopies permitted.
- Valid for one use only.
- Check with company for any shipping & handling costs.
- May not be combined with any other offer.

Atelier Homeschool Art

- Use original coupon; no photocopies permitted.
- Valid for one use only.
- Check with company for any shipping & handling costs.
- May not be combined with any other offer.

Math Drawings

- Use original coupon; no photocopies permitted.
- Valid for one use only.
- Check with company for any shipping & handling costs.
- May not be combined with any other offer.

Laurelwood Books

- Use original coupon; no photocopies permitted.
- Valid for one use only.
- Check with company for any shipping & handling costs.
- May not be combined with any other offer.

Tutor Lessons Interactive

- Use original coupon; no photocopies permitted.
- Valid for one use only.
- Check with company for any shipping & handling costs.
- May not be combined with any other offer.

e-TAP

- ◆ Use original coupon; no photocopies permitted.
- ◆ Valid for one use only.
- ◆ Check with company for any shipping & handling costs.
- ◆ May not be combined with any other offer.

TRISMS

- ◆ Use original coupon; no photocopies permitted.
- ◆ Valid for one use only.
- ◆ Check with company for any shipping & handling costs.
- ◆ May not be combined with any other offer.

Rethinking Education Conference

- ◆ Use original coupon; no photocopies permitted.
- ◆ Valid for one use only.
- ◆ Check with company for any shipping & handling costs.
- ◆ May not be combined with any other offer.

Sax Arts & Crafts

- ◆ Use original coupon; no photocopies permitted.
- ◆ Valid for one use only.
- ◆ Check with company for any shipping & handling costs.
- ◆ May not be combined with any other offer.

Scrap Stop

- ◆ Use original coupon; no photocopies permitted.
- ◆ Valid for one use only.
- ◆ Check with company for any shipping & handling costs.
- ◆ May not be combined with any other offer.

Teaching Tape

- ◆ Use original coupon; no photocopies permitted.
- ◆ Valid for one use only.
- ◆ Check with company for any shipping & handling costs.
- ◆ May not be combined with any other offer.

Homeschoolopoly

- Use original coupon;
  no photocopies permitted.
- Valid for one use only.
- Check with company for
  any shipping & handling costs.
- May not be combined with
  any other offer.

Family Tools

- Use original coupon;
  no photocopies permitted.
- Valid for one use only.
- Check with company for
  any shipping & handling costs.
- May not be combined with
  any other offer.

Homeschooling:
The Journey Is the Reward

- Use original coupon;
  no photocopies permitted.
- Valid for one use only.
- Check with company for
  any shipping & handling costs.
- May not be combined with
  any other offer.

Simply Music

- Use original coupon;
  no photocopies permitted.
- Valid for one use only.
- Check with company for
  any shipping & handling costs.
- May not be combined with
  any other offer.

Hollywood 101

- Use original coupon;
  no photocopies permitted.
- Valid for one use only.
- Check with company for
  any shipping & handling costs.
- May not be combined with
  any other offer.

Hollywood 101

- Use original coupon;
  no photocopies permitted.
- Valid for one use only.
- Check with company for
  any shipping & handling costs.
- May not be combined with
  any other offer.

Ampersand Press

- Use original coupon; no photocopies permitted.
- Valid for one use only.
- Check with company for any shipping & handling costs.
- May not be combined with any other offer.

Writing Strands

- Use original coupon; no photocopies permitted.
- Valid for one use only.
- Check with company for any shipping & handling costs.
- May not be combined with any other offer.

Boomerang Audio Magazine

- Use original coupon; no photocopies permitted.
- Valid for one use only.
- Check with company for any shipping & handling costs.
- May not be combined with any other offer.

Ring of Fire
Science Kits for Kids

- Use original coupon; no photocopies permitted.
- Valid for one use only.
- Check with company for any shipping & handling costs.
- May not be combined with any other offer.

Christian Technologies, Inc.

- Use original coupon; no photocopies permitted.
- Valid for one use only.
- Check with company for any shipping & handling costs.
- May not be combined with any other offer.

Greek 'n' Stuff

- Use original coupon; no photocopies permitted.
- Valid for one use only.
- Check with company for any shipping & handling costs.
- May not be combined with any other offer.

FergNus

- ◆ Use original coupon; no photocopies permitted.
- ◆ Valid for one use only.
- ◆ Check with company for any shipping & handling costs.
- ◆ May not be combined with any other offer.

E-Tutor

- ◆ Use original coupon; no photocopies permitted.
- ◆ Valid for one use only.
- ◆ Check with company for any shipping & handling costs.
- ◆ May not be combined with any other offer.

Greathall Productions

- ◆ Use original coupon; no photocopies permitted.
- ◆ Valid for one use only.
- ◆ Check with company for any shipping & handling costs.
- ◆ May not be combined with any other offer.

Lester Family Tapes

- ◆ Use original coupon; no photocopies permitted.
- ◆ Valid for one use only.
- ◆ Check with company for any shipping & handling costs.
- ◆ May not be combined with any other offer.

P.O. Box 55, Tranquility, CA 93668

The Link Homeschool Newspaper

- ◆ Use original coupon; no photocopies permitted.
- ◆ Valid for one use only.
- ◆ Check with company for any shipping & handling costs.
- ◆ May not be combined with any other offer.

Carschooling

- ◆ Use original coupon; no photocopies permitted.
- ◆ Valid for one use only.
- ◆ Check with company for any shipping & handling costs.
- ◆ May not be combined with any other offer.

Wordsmiths

- Use original coupon; no photocopies permitted.
- Valid for one use only.
- Check with company for any shipping & handling costs.
- May not be combined with any other offer.

StarrMatica

- Use original coupon; no photocopies permitted.
- Valid for one use only.
- Check with company for any shipping & handling costs.
- May not be combined with any other offer.

Cram School

- Use original coupon; no photocopies permitted.
- Valid for one use only.
- Check with company for any shipping & handling costs.
- May not be combined with any other offer.

Laser Typing

- Use original coupon; no photocopies permitted.
- Valid for one use only.
- Check with company for any shipping & handling costs.
- May not be combined with any other offer.

Five Finger Paragraph

- Use original coupon; no photocopies permitted.
- Valid for one use only.
- Check with company for any shipping & handling costs.
- May not be combined with any other offer.

Hexco

- Use original coupon; no photocopies permitted.
- Valid for one use only.
- Check with company for any shipping & handling costs.
- May not be combined with any other offer.

August House

- ◆ Use original coupon; no photocopies permitted.
- ◆ Valid for one use only.
- ◆ Check with company for any shipping & handling costs.
- ◆ May not be combined with any other offer.

Family Tools

- ◆ Use original coupon; no photocopies permitted.
- ◆ Valid for one use only.
- ◆ Check with company for any shipping & handling costs.
- ◆ May not be combined with any other offer.

Academic Superstore

- ◆ Use original coupon; no photocopies permitted.
- ◆ Valid for one use only.
- ◆ Check with company for any shipping & handling costs.
- ◆ May not be combined with any other offer.

Day to Day

- ◆ Use original coupon; no photocopies permitted.
- ◆ Valid for one use only.
- ◆ Check with company for any shipping & handling costs.
- ◆ May not be combined with any other offer.

Christian Liberty Press

- ◆ Use original coupon; no photocopies permitted.
- ◆ Valid for one use only.
- ◆ Check with company for any shipping & handling costs.
- ◆ May not be combined with any other offer.

Adoremus Books

- ◆ Use original coupon; no photocopies permitted.
- ◆ Valid for one use only.
- ◆ Check with company for any shipping & handling costs.
- ◆ May not be combined with any other offer.

Index